AF378526

Walks in the Midlands Countryside

around Birmingham and the Black Country: Tracing the Journeys of a 19th Century Writer

Brian Conduit

© Brian Conduit, 2013

All Rights Reserved. No part of this publication may be reproduced, stored in a retrieval system, or transmitted in any form or by any means – electronic, mechanical, photocopying, recording, or otherwise – without prior written permission from the publisher or a licence permitting restricted copying issued by the Copyright Licensing Agency, 90 Tottenham Court Road, London W1P 0LA. This book may not be lent, resold, hired out or otherwise disposed of by trade in any form of binding or cover other than that in which it is published, without the prior consent of the publisher.

Moral Rights: The author has asserted his moral right to be indentified as the Author of this Work.

Published by Sigma Leisure – an imprint of
Sigma Press, Stobart House, Pontyclerc, Penybanc Road, Ammanford, Carmarthenshire SA18 3HP.

British Library Cataloguing in Publication Data
A CIP record for this book is available from the British Library.

ISBN: 978-1-85058-971-6

Typesetting and Design by: Sigma Press, Ammanford.

Cover photographs: Brian Conduit. Top, left to right: Brewood from the canal, Anne Hathaway's Cottage at Shottery, The Four Stones, on top of the Clent Hills; Main photograph: Extensive ruins of Wenlock Priory

Photographs: Brian Conduit

Maps: Rebecca Terry

Printed by: TJ International, Padstow, Cornwall

Disclaimer: the information in this book is given in good faith and is believed to be correct at the time of publication. No responsibility is accepted by either the author or publisher for errors or omissions, or for any loss or injury howsoever caused. Only you can judge your own fitness, competence and experience. Do not reply solely on sketch maps for navigation: we strongly recommend the use of appropriate Ordnance Survey (or equivalent) maps.

Preface

In 1865 Elihu Burritt, a notable American peace and anti-slavery activist, was appointed the United States consul in Birmingham, at the time a rapidly growing manufacturing city and centre of a major industrial area. He carried out his duties in a most conscientious manner, submitting regular reports to the Department of State in Washington and travelling extensively throughout the Midlands, not just in Birmingham and the heavily industrialised Black Country but also in the rural areas that lay beyond the industrial belt in Warwickshire, Worcestershire, Staffordshire and Shropshire. Burritt was full of enthusiasm for everything he saw and his obvious love for the area shines through on virtually every page of the book that he subsequently wrote about his journeys. That book, published in 1868, was entitled *Walks in the Black Country and its Green Borderland*'

Despite its title, Burritt's book was not a walking guide but a general account of his travels, the people he met and his enquiries, comments and observations on the current state of the region. In contrast this book is a walking guide but is not about the built-up industrial Midlands i.e. the city of Birmingham and the Black Country. Instead it concentrates on the 'green borderland' as Burritt called it, the pleasant rural areas that encircle the industrial zone, revisiting most of the places that he journeyed to in the 1860s and attempting to retrace some of his walks.

Inevitably much has changed. Elihu Burritt would undoubtedly find intolerable the noise of the motorways and other busy main roads that thread their way across the region and he would probably lament the suburban sprawl that has obliterated many areas on the fringes of the conurbation which in his day would still have been open and unspoilt countryside. One modern development that would certainly bemuse him and which he would fine difficult to comprehend is the designation of the Ironbridge Gorge, one of the most important industrial locations in the Midlands in the mid-19th century, as a UNESCO World Heritage Site, now visited by thousands of tourists as a major historic attraction rather than as a world renowned pioneering and innovative centre of industry. .

At the same time although much has changed, much has also remained relatively unaltered and these 20 walks take you through areas of the

Midlands which, 150 years since Burritt walked this way, still contain some of the most varied, beautiful and interesting landscapes and some of the finest old towns and villages in the country.

Contents

Walk Location Map
N
Stoke-on-Trent
M5
Oswestry
Market Drayton
Stafford
Shrewsbury
Telford
2
1
7
8
9
10
Lichfield
M6 Toll
4
5
6
M54
3
M42
Wolverhampton
19
Dudley
Birmingham
18
20
M6
16
17
Coventry
Ludlow
15
Solihull
11
12
Kidderminster
Warwick
13
M40
Worcester
14
Stratford-upon-Avon
Hereford
Ledbury
1   Walk Reference Number
The Midlands Boundary (Includes the counties of Shropshire, Staffordshire, West Midlands, Warwickshire, Worcestershire & Herefordshire)

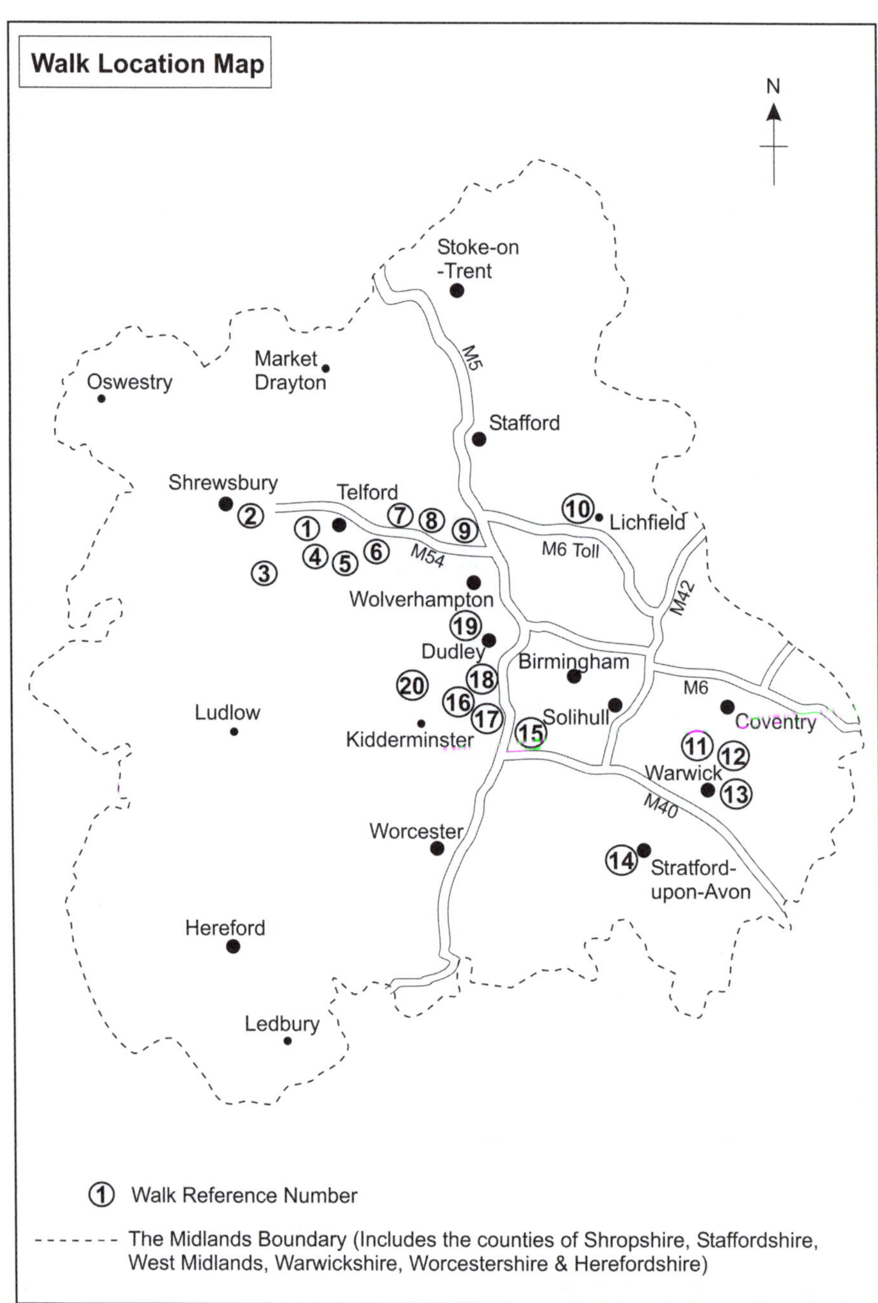

6

Introduction

This book is a collection of 20 walks in the attractive countryside of the West Midlands that surrounds the built up area of Birmingham and the Black Country, extending over parts of rural Shropshire, Staffordshire, Warwickshire and Worcestershire. The inspiration for it is a uniquely fascinating book called 'Walks in the Black Country and its Green Borderland', written in 1868 by Elihu Burritt, the American consul in Birmingham at the time.

Elihu Burritt was a man of humble background, born in New Britain, Connecticut, USA in 1810. At the age of sixteen he was apprenticed to a blacksmith but his enormous thirst for knowledge and appetite for books soon earned him the nickname the 'learned blacksmith'. In time this totally self-taught man developed a remarkable fluency in many languages and became a well-known and respected crusader for world peace. He travelled widely throughout America and Europe, attending several international congresses and writing numerous books, articles and pamphlets. He also actively supported other worthy causes, including the anti-slavery campaign in America, the temperance movement and the promotion of a cheap universal postal system. His support for the latter was based on the grounds that he believed that greater communication amongst peoples and nations could reduce the likelihood of future war.

It was on the basis of such activities and his obvious enthusiasm and capacity for hard work that in 1865 President Lincoln appointed him the United States Consul in Birmingham. During his five years in that job he lived at Harborne, now a pleasant residential suburb of Birmingham but then still a rural village. His house, which he named New Britain Villa after his American birthplace, still stands in Victoria Road. While there he immersed himself in worthy causes and local activities, worshipping at Harborne's medieval church and vigorously supporting its restoration. In his book he describes the congregation coming 'across the broad fields that converge from every direction into the solemn aisles of the churchyard trees'. Even today this part of Harborne retains much of its previous village atmosphere with the old church flanked by a bowling green and the Bell Inn.

In the course of his consular duties Burritt travelled extensively throughout the region, meeting industrialists, clergymen, local councillors, farmers, factory workers, landowners and many others. His book was an account of these journeys, in which he hoped – in the author's own words in the preface – 'to give distant readers a bird's-eye view of the district of which it treats, and, perhaps, present a few points and aspects of interest which some persons residing within it may have overlooked'.

Many people who know little about either Elihu Burritt himself or his book might be familiar with its first sentence, the most famous quotation from it which is prominently displayed at the Black Country Museum near Dudley and which perfectly sums up the appearance and significance of the area at the time. 'The Black Country, black by day and red by night, cannot be matched, for vast and varied production, by any other space of equal radius on the surface of the globe'.

After a brief introduction, the first part of the book is about Birmingham, its history, great men (scientists, industrialists, politicians, artists and clergymen), institutions, public buildings and in particular its rapidly expanding industries. Then Burritt goes on to give details of the chief towns and industries of the Black Country and it is in the final chapters that he describes his visits and walks in the 'green borderland', the rural areas around the industrial zone.

Burritt was fascinated and intrigued both by the growing city of Birmingham and its most notable citizens and by the Black Country, then approaching the zenith of its industrial greatness, but he was equally if not more enthusiastic about the unspoilt countryside surrounding the industrial area. He described it in these words: 'The Black Country is beautifully framed by a Green Borderland; and that border is rich and redolent with two beautiful wealths – the sweet life of Nature's happiest springs and summers, and the hive and romance of England's happiest industries'.

If such words seem to be somewhat over the top, that is a trait that appears throughout the book. Like many Victorian English writers Elihu Burritt was inclined to get carried away by his own enthusiasm – an admirable quality in many ways – and this led him to indulge in frequent over-exaggeration. Two other examples of his purple prose are his comparison of the Lickey Hills with the Scottish Highlands ('these remarkable hills look as if transported from the Highlands….they are perfectly Scotch in cut and clothing') and his description of the view from the summit of the Wrekin ('The hill-top...is not only a grand point of observation but of reflection, commanding landscapes of a wonderful extent and variety and scenes of historical interest').

He rather goes to town in his descriptions of some of the suburbs of Birmingham as well. He writes: 'Moseley, Edgbaston and Harborne......are as goodly suburbs as any town in England can show. Hills, dales, gentle slopes, valleys and streams, make a picturesque scenery. The residences of many of the prosperous businessmen of the borough are interspersed in the landscape, and the ornamental grounds form a pleasant feature. Edgbaston especially is full of these elegant houses and gardens'. As someone who lived for the first 21 years of his life in one of those suburbs and walked and cycled extensively through all three of them, I have to say that, despite the exaggerated phraseology, much of what he wrote in the 1860s fortunately still applies today to these areas of the city.

On most of his walks Burritt was accompanied by the Devon-born poet, Edward Capern, who was also a resident of Harborne at the time. Like Burritt he was a self-taught man – he had been a postman in his native Devon – with a thirst for knowledge. So the 'learned blacksmith' and 'postman poet' made a particularly well-suited pair on their long walks around the Midlands.

In the book Burritt describes their walking routine which most walkers would find somewhat unusual. For a start they did most of their walks during November, not usually regarded as the best time of the year for any outdoor activities in this country. Also they started late in the day, which seems a strange time to embark on long walks when the days are at their shortest. After breakfast Burritt would spend the morning writing up his previous day's observations, then they would take a light lunch around noon and walk until dusk, often not reaching the place they had come to see until after dark. Moreover the weather always seemed to be fine, even in late November, which again is not the general experience of most people who venture out into the Midlands countryside at that time of year. Almost every walk is prefaced by such comments as: 'a day brimful of the rich glory of an autumn sun', and 'the weather was beautiful and all the scenery was rich with the golden glory of autumn, and on a beautiful afternoon of the last of November'.

Surprisingly for someone born in New England, a part of the United States renowned above all else for the beauty of its fall, Burritt frequently comments that autumn was his favourite season in England. In one passage he states that 'The scenery in England in the autumn cannot be equalled by that of any other country' and in another – on this occasion while admiring the view from the Wrekin – he enthuses: 'The mellowest sun in an English autumn was descending the western horizon and no other autumn sun the wide world round equals it'.

Elihu Burritt was an exceptionally interesting, curious, meticulous and talented man and his book 'Walks in the Black Country and Its Green Borderland' strongly conveys the way of life of an important region of Britain around the middle of the 19th century, at a time when it was rapidly expanding into one of the foremost industrial areas of the world and when Britain was at the height of its industrial supremacy. As such it is much more than a description of walks in the countryside, villages and towns of the Midlands but an invaluable, detailed and absorbing source of economic and social history.

The aim of this book is to revisit most of the areas of the 'green borderland' that Burritt visited, seeing how much has changed and how much has remained largely unaltered since his time. Tracing his exact journeys is not always possible as his book was not a walking guide and he rarely gave precise route directions. Therefore most of the routes are a matter of conjecture. Also trying to trace his exact routes is not always desirable as in many instances he would have undoubtedly made use of country lanes rather than footpaths which at the time would have been little more than cart tracks but now will have become busy roads.

A glance at a map reveals that the walks are distributed all around the Midlands, with a heavy concentration in Shropshire, a county that Burritt refers to frequently. The walks are fairly easy and of modest length, well within the capabilities of most and generally considerably shorter than his routes. On many of his journeys he began by walking through open country on the edge of Birmingham to reach the main objective of his walks. Now much of that open country has become covered by suburban housing and the routes in this guide avoid this and mostly start in the rural locations themselves. Burritt and his walking companion Capern only made use of public transport when travelling by rail out of Birmingham.

While sampling these 20 walks, it is to be hoped that walkers will experience a selection of enjoyable and interesting expeditions in the countryside around Birmingham and the Black Country and will reach the conclusion that, 150 years after Burritt's journeys, it is still a highly attractive 'green borderland'. Also perhaps some will have their appetites whetted to read the whole of Elihu Burritt's book, a fascinating glimpse into this part of the country during the Victorian era provided by a sympathetic and highly enthusiastic foreigner.

General Information

Useful Organisations
The Ramblers' Association, 2nd Floor Camelford House, 87-90 Albert Embankment, London SE1 7TW Tel: 020 7339 8500
ramblers@ramblers.org.uk
The National Trust, Heelis Building, Kemble Drive, Swindon, Wiltshire Tel: 01793 817400 **enquiries@nationaltrust.org.uk**
English Heritage, 1 Waterhouse Square, 138-142 Holborn, London EC19 2ST Tel: 020 7973 3000   **customers@english-heritage.org.uk**
West Midlands Regional Office, English Heritage, The Axis, 10 Holliday Street, Birmingham B1 1TG Tel: 0121 625 6820
west.midlands@english-heritage.org.uk

Public Transport
For information about public transport contact Traveline either by visiting www.traveline.org.uk or phoning 0871 200 2233. Alternatively you could contact the local visitor information centre.

Maps
The sketch maps in this book are only a rough guide and you should always take with you the relevant Ordnance Survey map. The most suitable ones for walkers are the Explorer maps and the following cover this area.
        205 (Stratford-upon-Avon & Evesham)
        217 (The Long Mynd & Wenlock Edge)
        218 (Wyre Forest & Kidderminster)
        219 (Wolverhampton & Dudley)
        220 (Birmingham)

221 (Coventry & Warwick)
232 (Nuneaton & Tamworth)
242 (Telford, Ironbridge & The Wrekin)
244 (Cannock Chase & Chasewater)

Visitor Information Centres

The following are in the area covered by this guide

Birmingham 0844 888 3883
visit@marketingbirmingham.com

Ironbridge   01952 884391
tic@ironbridge.org.uk

Kenilworth   01926 748900
kenilworthlibrary@warwickshire.gov.uk

Leamington 0870 160 7930
leamington@shakespeare-country.co.uk

Lichfield 01543 412121
info@visitlichfield.com

Much Wenlock 01952 727679
muchwenlock.tourism@shropshire-cc.gov.uk

Stratford-upon-Avon 01789 264293
tic@discover-stratford.com

Telford 01952 238008
tourist-info@telfordshopping.co.uk

Warwick 01926 492212
touristinfo@warwick-uk.co.uk

1. The Wrekin

'A view of heaven and earth at that moment beautiful and glorious'

Distance	4 miles (6.4 km)
Approximate time	2½ hours
Start	The Wrekin and The Ercall car park, on minor road about 1 ½ miles to the south west of Wellington town centre, grid ref SJ637094
Parking	At the start
Terrain	Steady climb to the summit followed by a steeper descent, clear paths and tracks throughout and much of the route through woodland
Refreshments	None, apart from light refreshments sometimes at the Halfway House
Public Transport	None
Map	OS Explorer 242 (Telford, Ironbridge & The Wrekin)

It is no wonder that Elihu Burritt waxed lyrical over the view from the summit of The Wrekin as this isolated hill, rising to 1335 feet (407m) above a predominantly flat landscape, provides a succession of glorious and unimpeded views. Its distinctive conical shape also makes it a commanding presence in that landscape, visible for miles around. This walk is the only one in the book where it is possible to more or less trace Burritt's exact route as it is one of the few occasions where he gives precise route details. The main difference between this walk and the one that he did with his companion, the poet Edward Capern, is that they began their walk from Wellington station, to where they had caught a train from Birmingham, whereas this walk is shorter and avoids a lot of urban road walking by starting from a car park conveniently situated at the foot of the hill. The ascent is steady and quite lengthy; the descent is shorter but much steeper and therefore those not used to hill walking might prefer to retrace their steps from the summit to the start. Try and choose a good day for this walk in order to enjoy the views at their best.

The Walk

1. Turn right out of the car park along the lane, in the Shrewsbury direction, and after a few yards, turn sharp left through a gate onto a track. The ascent begins immediately with a steady climb through the trees that clothe the slopes of The Wrekin. At a Shropshire Way sign, follow the main track around a sharp right bend and continue to a waymarked stile by the Halfway House. Burritt describes this building as a 'large cottage planted at a good point of view'. He also mentions that it provided refreshments, a role it still on occasions serves today. After climbing the stile, keep ahead to a fork and take the main track which bends left – there is another Shropshire Way sign here – and continues up to emerge into more open country where it levels off. An information board indicates when you have reached Hell Gate, the outer entrance to an Iron Age fort, and you continue a little further on up to the obvious earthworks of Heaven Gate, where you pass through the inner entrance to the fort. From here it is just a short distance to the cairn and trig point at the summit.

The wooded track that ascends The Wrekin

Walk 1
N
500m
Reservoir
To Wellington
P
1
Wrekin Cottage
To Uppington
Hell Gate
Heaven Gate
The Wrekin
Wenlocks Wood
White Cottage Plantation
Summit 407m
2
Gibbons Coppice
Little Hill
3
To Little Wenlock

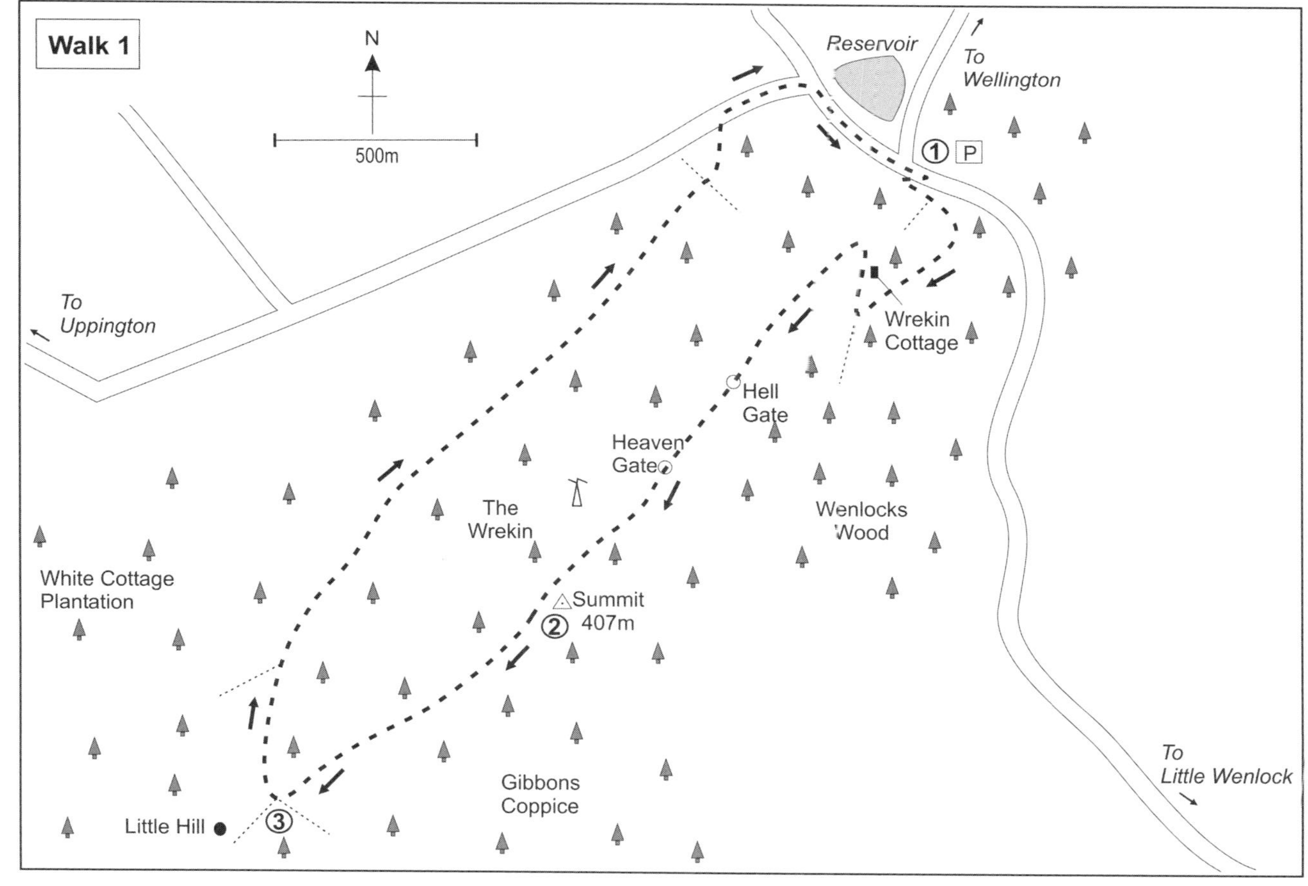

15

The summit of The Wrekin is 1335 feet (407m) high and the magnificent all round views more than compensate for the effort made to reach this point. The views overlook the broad lowlands of the Severn valley with the Shropshire hills on the horizon and – in clear conditions – extend in a wide arc from the edge of the Black Country in the east across to the mountains of north Wales in the west, a huge slice of the country. Not surprisingly Burritt's purple prose really comes to the fore at such a viewpoint. Here is one brief example: 'It opened up a view of heaven and earth at that moment beautiful and glorious, beyond the genius of poet or painter to picture to a distant eye...we looked off into the great valley, north, south, and west. It was a vast basin filled with autumnal glory that ran over the brim on all sides. From the height on which we stood, a hundred smaller hills sank almost to the levels of the common fields that floored the great amphitheatre with their living mosaic'.

Extensive views from the summit of The Wrekin

2. From the summit either retrace your steps to the start if you want to avoid the steep descent; otherwise keep ahead past the summit cairn, heading down to pass through the far entrance of the fort. Continue steadily downhill across an open landscape before descending steeply through woodland on a stony path to a crossways just before reaching the bottom.

3. Turn right along a track which curves to the right along the lower slopes of the hill and descends to a T-junction. Turn right onto a path and at a fork, keep ahead along the left hand path. The route is still following that taken by Burritt and Capern, returning along the western base of the hill. This undulating path maintains a fairly straight line through the trees to reach a redundant stile. Pass beside it and keep ahead, taking the left hand path at any forks, to eventually emerge onto a lane. Turn right and at a T-junction turn right again for the short distance back to the car park.

2. Around Wroxeter

'Hidden among the green growths of a modern civilisation, lies buried the old Roman Uriconium, once a goodly city under several Roman emperors'

Distance	5½ miles (8.9 km)
Approximate time	2½ hours
Start	Wroxeter, on the B4380 6 miles south east of Shrewsbury, grid ref SJ565088
Parking	English Heritage car park at Wroxeter (parking charge refunded when you visit the Roman site)
Terrain	Quiet roads and clear field paths and tracks across flat terrain
Refreshments	Pub about 1 mile (1.6 km) after the start
Public Transport	Buses from Shrewsbury and Telford
Map	OS Explorer 241 (Shrewsbury)

Elihu Burritt only refers to the Roman city of Uriconium (present day Wroxeter) while enthusing on the view from the summit of The Wrekin but his detailed description and knowledge of the site suggests that he probably visited it. The walk is a circuit of the pleasant countryside to the east of the River Severn and the wide, extensive and unimpeded views throughout across the flat and gently undulating terrain of the valley are dominated inevitably by the distinctive profile of The Wrekin.

The Walk

Wroxeter or Viroconium (now the preferred Latin name for the town rather than Uriconium) was originally founded as a legionary fortress in the 1st century AD. After the legions moved to Chester, it later developed into a prosperous civilian settlement and at one time was the fourth largest city in Roman Britain. Most of it still remains under the surrounding fields and it is only the public baths complex that has been excavated. However the remains that can be seen, mostly dating from the 2nd century, are among the most impressive in Britain. Particularly outstanding is the Old Work, the wall that separates the basilica from the public baths, which is one of the largest and tallest freestanding pieces of Roman masonry in the country. Adjoining the public baths are the excavated remains of the market hall and shops. There is evidence that Wroxeter continued in use well after the end of the Roman occupation in the early 5th century but unlike many towns in England of Roman origin, it never became an important place in the Anglo-Saxon and medieval periods and appears to have been abandoned sometime in the 7th century. The first real excavation of the site took place in 1859, only a few years before Elihu Burritt came this way.

The impressive remains of the Roman city of Viroconium

Walk 2
To Telford →
To Shrewsbury
B4394
B5061
Norton
Horseshoe Inn
Bell Brook
①
②
Rebuilt Roman Villa
Viroconivm Roman Town
P
Beslow Cottages
Roman Wall
Wroxeter
Donnington
River Severn
N
500m
Eyton on Severn
③

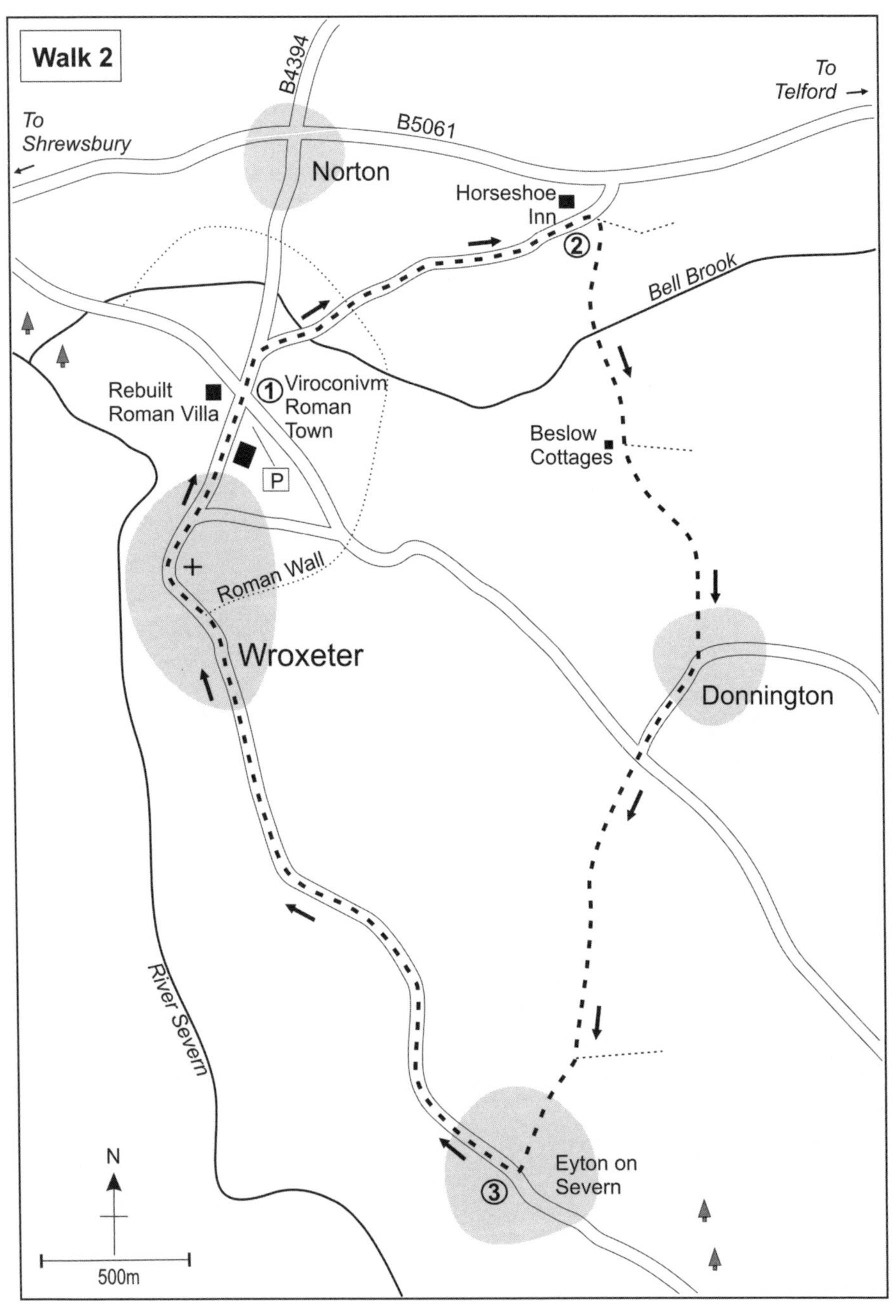

20

Recently a replica Roman town house has been built on the site of the forum, using Roman materials and building techniques. Its construction was shown in a series of television programmes on Channel 4 and it gives a striking insight into what town life was like in Roman Britain. Lining the road in front of it are the bases of some of the columns of the forum.

1. Turn right out of the car park to a crossroads and keep ahead, in the Norton and Walcot direction. Take the first lane on the right and after ¾ mile (1.2 km) you reach the Horseshoe Inn.

2. At a public bridleway sign, turn right in front of the pub and walk along a tarmac track. This soon becomes a rough, enclosed, winding track which you follow to a cottage where the track bends left. Keep ahead through a gate and continue along the right edge of the next two fields. About half way along the second field, look out for a public bridleway sign which directs you to bear left across the field. On the

The distinctive bulk of The Wrekin can be seen from many points on the walk

far side, turn right onto a straight track, eventually bearing right in front of a house to a lane in the hamlet of Donnington. Bear right along it to a T-junction, cross over and keep ahead along a track by the right edge of a field. Continue along the right edge of a series of fields, going through a succession of gates, until you bear right on joining an enclosed track. Follow it to a road in the hamlet of Eyton on Severn.

3. Turn right and follow the road for 1 ½ miles (2.4 km) into the small and secluded village that is present day Wroxeter. Walk past the medieval church, partly built from stones acquired from the ruins of the Roman city, and continue along the road for just under ½ mile (800m) to return to the car park.

Village church at Wroxeter

3. Wenlock Edge

'Its old abbey ruin with its ranks of pillars and arches'

Distance	**3½ miles (5.6 km)**
Approximate time	**2 hours**
Start	**Much Wenlock, The Square, grid ref SO624999**
Parking	**Much Wenlock**
Terrain	**Easy walking mainly across fields and through woodland; one steady climb onto Wenlock Edge**
Refreshments	**Pubs and cafes at Much Wenlock**
Public Transport	**Buses from Shrewsbury, Bridgnorth and Ironbridge**
Map	**OS Explorers 217 (The Long Mynd & Wenlock Edge) and 242 (Telford, Ironbridge & The Wrekin)**

Like Wroxeter and Ironbridge, Elihu Burritt only refers to Much Wenlock and its monastic remains while enthusing on the view that rewards him after his ascent of The Wrekin. From the centre of Much Wenlock the walk leads, via a steady and easy climb mainly along a sunken track, onto the wooded ridge of Wenlock Edge. A short walk along the edge brings grand views over the Shropshire countryside and this is followed by a gentle descent back into the small town, reaching the centre opposite the extensive ruins of the priory that Burritt so admired.

The Walk

The small, attractive town of Much Wenlock is situated at the foot of Wenlock Edge, a wooded ridge that extends south westwards from here across Shropshire to Craven Arms. Its centre is dominated by the fine medieval church, which dates from the 12th century, and the 16th century, timber-framed guildhall.

1. Start in The Square and walk along High Street away from the town centre. At a road junction keep ahead along the A458 and where the main road bears right, turn left along a road signposted to Church Stretton and Wenlock Edge.

2. At signs for public bridleway and Blakeway Hollow, turn right onto a tarmac track and head up to a gate just beyond the last of the houses. After climbing a stile to the side of the gate, the route continues steadily uphill along a hedge-lined track for the next ½ mile (0.8 km). Shortly after the track levels off, it bends sharply to the left and at a footpath post just before entering the woodland, turn right through a gate. Keep ahead across a field to a stile.

Church and Guildhall at Much Wenlock

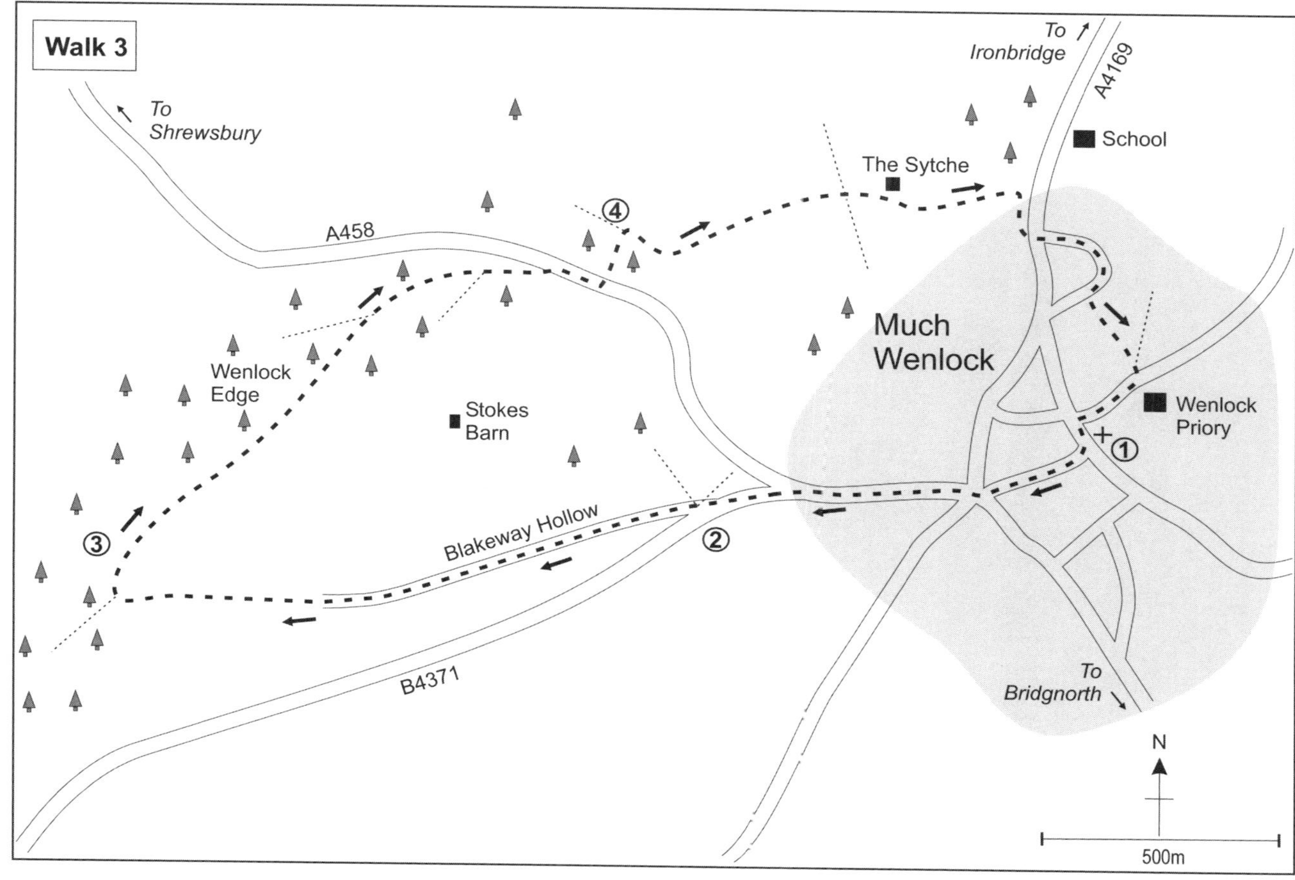

Walk 3
To Ironbridge
A4169
School
The Sytche
To Shrewsbury
A458
Much Wenlock
Wenlock Edge
Stokes Barn
Wenlock Priory
Blakeway Hollow
B4371
To Bridgnorth
N
500m
1
2
3
4

3. Climb it and turn right onto a path between a fence on the right and the edge of the woodland that crowns the ridge of Wenlock Edge on the left. Go through two gates in quick succession, keep ahead and in the field corner, turn left through two more gates. Turn right and continue through the wood, descending steps into a hollow, heading up again and continuing along a winding track to another gate. Go through and keep ahead through another gate to emerge onto a road. Turn right – take care as this is a busy road and there are no verges – and after about 100 yards (91m), turn left through a kissing gate, at a public footpath sign, and walk along a woodland track.

4. In front of a gate, turn right onto a path that keeps initially by the left inside edge of the trees and later along the right edge of a field. Follow the curve of the field edge to the left, go through a kissing gate in the corner and continue along the right edge of a caravan site. After

Extensive ruins of Wenlock Priory

joining a track, keep along it to emerge onto a road on the edge of Much Wenlock and continue to a T-junction. Turn right, take the first road on the left (Station Road) and follow the road to the right in front of the former station building. Just before reaching a 30 mph sign, turn left onto a path by a hedge on the left and continue along a straight, fence-lined path which emerges, via a kissing gate, onto a lane in front of the ruins of Wenlock Priory.

Despite Elihu Burritt referring to it as an abbey, the monastic house here was a Cluniac priory, as were all houses belonging to the Cluniac Order. There was originally a Saxon abbey on the site but this was refounded as a Cluniac priory by Roger of Montgomery, Earl of Shrewsbury, soon after the Norman Conquest. Most of the remains date from the 13th century and include the south side of the nave and south transept of the church, plus the splendid chapter house. After the dissolution of the priory in 1540, the prior's house and infirmary were converted into a private residence. In the attractive and peaceful garden there are some fine examples of topiary work.

Turn right along the lane and at a T-junction, turn left, passing the church and guildhall, to return to The Square.

4. Ironbridge and Coalbrookdale

What village or hamlet in the United States has not some memento of Coalbrookdale?'

Distance	**4 miles (6.4 km)**
Approximate time	**2 ½ hours**
Start	**Ironbridge, on the south side of the Iron Bridge, grid ref SJ672034**
Parking	**Ironbridge**
Terrain	**Field and woodland paths, some road walking, several climbs including flights of steps**
Refreshments	**Pubs and cafes at Ironbridge, pubs at Coalbrookdale, cafe at the Museum of Iron at Coalbrookdale**
Public Transport	**Buses from Telford, Much Wenlock and Shrewsbury**
Map	**OS Explorer 242 (Telford, Ironbridge & The Wrekin)**

One of the surprising features of Elihu Burritt's book is that, apart from the quotations used after the headings for this walk and the next one, he hardly mentions Coalbrookdale and never refers to Ironbridge at all. Although the Ironbridge area had declined from its 18th century heyday as industries moved away to the more plentiful supplies of minerals and better transport links in the nearby Black Country, it was still one of the most famous and iconic industrial areas in the world. However it is more than likely that he did visit it as part of his consular duties as its industries would have been of greater interest to the US government than the views from the Clent Hills or the architectural qualities of Lichfield Cathedral. This walk is full of both historic interest and scenic beauty, taking in the

Iron Bridge itself and the Museum of Iron at Coalbrookdale, plus attractive areas of woodland, grassland and grand views over the gorge.

The Walk

The Ironbridge Gorge is often described as the 'birthplace of the Industrial Revolution'. This is largely because it was here in 1709 that Abraham Darby, a local ironmaster, first successfully smelted iron ore by using coke instead of the traditional charcoal. This revolutionised the iron industry by freeing it from its dependence on timber (supplies were becoming depleted whereas coal was plentiful) and making it possible to produce much greater quantities more cheaply. In turn this revolutionised British industry as a whole by enabling the large scale production of all things iron – machine parts, tools, rail tracks, boilers, domestic utensils, etc.. This is the historical significance of the Ironbridge Gorge and the reason why it is one of Britain's UNESCO World Heritage sites and has become a popular tourist destination.

Once the gorge had become a major industrial area, there was a demand from local industrialists, led by Abraham Darby III, for improved transport links, in particular for the construction of a new bridge across the Severn. The Iron Bridge, the first of its kind in the world, was completed in 1779 and aroused universal interest. Over the following decades people came from all over Europe and beyond to see this wonder of the age and triumph of British engineering. Nowadays it is the focal point of a series of ten museums and other related industrial sites scattered throughout the Severn gorge and the adjacent valley of Coalbrookdale.

1. Start by crossing the Iron Bridge into the town of the same name which grew up on its north side and climb the flight of steps just to the right of the Tontine Inn. At the top turn left along the road, passing the church on the left, take the right hand upper road at a fork and head gently uphill, curving gradually to the right. At the next fork, turn sharp left – there is a public footpath sign – along a track, almost doubling back, and at the next public footpath sign, turn right onto a woodland path. Bear right at a junction of paths, in the Paradise direction, heading gently downhill, and at the next fingerpost a short distance ahead, bear left, again following directions to Paradise, and continue more steeply downhill to a crossways. Keep ahead, descend

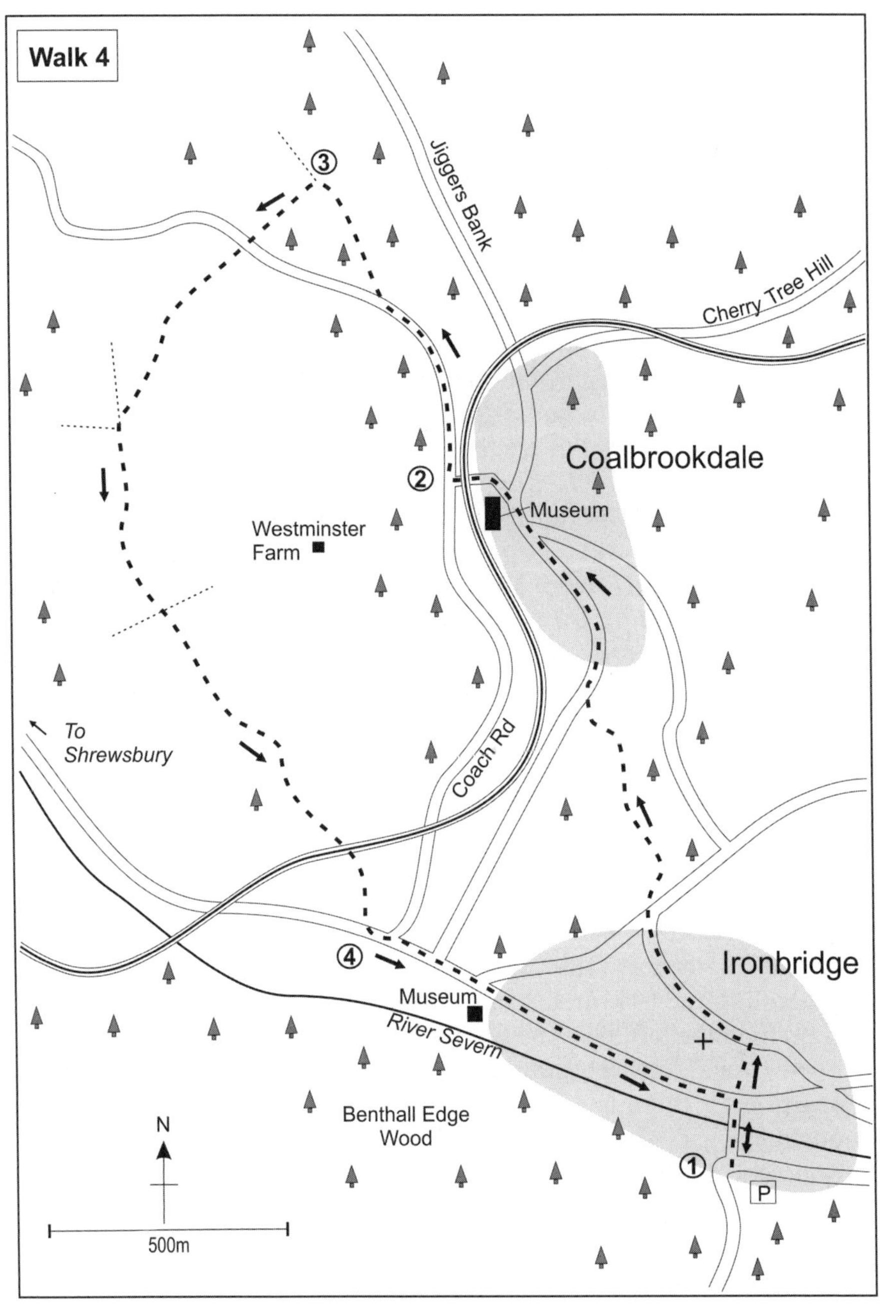

Walk 4
Jiggers Bank
Cherry Tree Hill
Coalbrookdale
Museum
Westminster Farm
To Shrewsbury
Coach Rd
Ironbridge
Museum
River Severn
Benthall Edge Wood
N
500m
P

The Iron Bridge, focal point of a series of historic sites in the Ironbridge Gorge

steps and at the bottom, continue along a path to a track. Turn left down to a lane and turn right to join the main road through Coalbrookdale. At a fork opposite Church Road, turn left downhill to the Museum of Iron and walk through the museum complex to the Old Furnace.

The Museum of Iron is on the site of the furnace where Abraham Darby first successfully smelted iron ore with coke in 1709. The Old Furnace where this happened can be seen at the far end of the open area, protected from the elements by a modern building. Its huge importance obviously makes it one of the major monuments of the early industrial age. Over the century and a half following this revolutionary technological breakthrough, the works produced a wide range of iron goods and, as Burritt's quotation indicates, became well known throughout the world. In the museum there are displays and artefacts

The Old Furnace at Coalbrookdale, protected by a modern building

chronicling the history of the iron industry in Coalbrookdale, plus a shop and café.

2. Head up to a track on the left alongside the site, by former railway arches, bear left under an arch and continue along a road to a T-junction. Turn left uphill, passing below the Darby Houses on the left, former homes of the family of ironmasters. At a public footpath sign to Ropewalk, pass beside a gate, continue along a track through woodland, part of an old horse-drawn tramway, and after going through another gate, keep ahead along the edge of a meadow.

3. At a public footpath sign to Holly Bank, turn left over a stile and head uphill along a path that keeps by the right inside edge of woodland. Climb a stile, keep ahead along an enclosed path and go through a gate onto a lane by the side of a house. Cross over, climb a stile and keep along the left edge of the next three fields, climbing a series of stiles. On entering the fourth field, bear left and walk across it, making for a stile. In front is a striking and not unattractive view of the pink cooling towers of Ironbridge Power Station down in the gorge. Climb the stile, maintain the same direction across the corner of the next field, climb

another stile in a hedge gap and turn left along a left field edge. Follow the curve of the field edge first to the right and then to the left, pass through a gap into the next field and continue along the left edge of the next two fields before continuing downhill through woodland. At the bottom of the hill, keep ahead along the left inside edge of the trees to a gate, go through and continue gently downhill along an

Pink cooling stations of Ironbridge power station

enclosed path to emerge onto a track. Keep along it, passing in front of a pair of houses, cross a railway line and continue down a track to a road.

4. Turn left and follow the road into Ironbridge, passing the Museum of the Gorge.

This museum, housed in the Old Severn Warehouse, tells the history of the Ironbridge Gorge and includes a model showing what the area would have been like at the end of the 18th century. Finally turn right and cross the Iron Bridge to return to the start.

5. Ironbridge, Jackfield and Coalport

'Whoever heard its name pronounced without thinking of a sad-iron or an iron porridge-pot?'

Distance	4 miles (6.4 km)
Approximate time	2 hours
Start	Ironbridge, on the south side of the Iron Bridge, grid ref SJ672034
Parking	Ironbridge
Terrain	Flat riverside walk on roads and paths to start with followed by some gentle climbing through woodland on the return leg
Refreshments	Pubs and cafes at Ironbridge, pub at Jackfield, pub at Coalport
Public Transport	Buses from Telford, Much Wenlock and Shrewsbury
Map	OS Explorer 242 (Telford, Ironbridge & The Wrekin)

Such is the wealth of historic attractions and places of interest in the Ironbridge Gorge that it merits two walks. This one takes you first along the south bank of the Severn to Jackfield and then across the river into Coalport. Both of these places were integral parts of the Ironbridge area during its industrial heyday. The return on the north side of the river is mostly through the beautiful woodland of Lloyds Coppice before a final stretch along the road into the town. The route passes close to three of the many museums scattered throughout the gorge.

The Walk

1. Begin by walking away from the bridge to the far end of the car park where you pick up a tree-lined track, part of the Severn Valley Way,

which runs between the road on the right and River Severn on the left. After going through a gate, keep ahead along a stretch of tarmac track to a road and continue along it, following signs to Tile Museum, Maws Craft Centre and Blists Hill Museums. Walk past the Jackfield Tile Museum where you bear left to continue along Church Road.

In the Jackfield Tile Museum there are examples of all kinds of tiles plus a series of rooms that show how they were displayed in various locations e.g. homes, railway stations, hospitals etc. There are also displays on the methods of production.

At the end of the road, keep ahead along a path through trees, which runs parallel to the river, to emerge onto a track, bear slightly right and head up to a road. Keep ahead and on reaching the Maws Craft Centre, turn left, at a signpost to Blists Hill Museums. Turn right onto

Ironbridge from the south side of the river

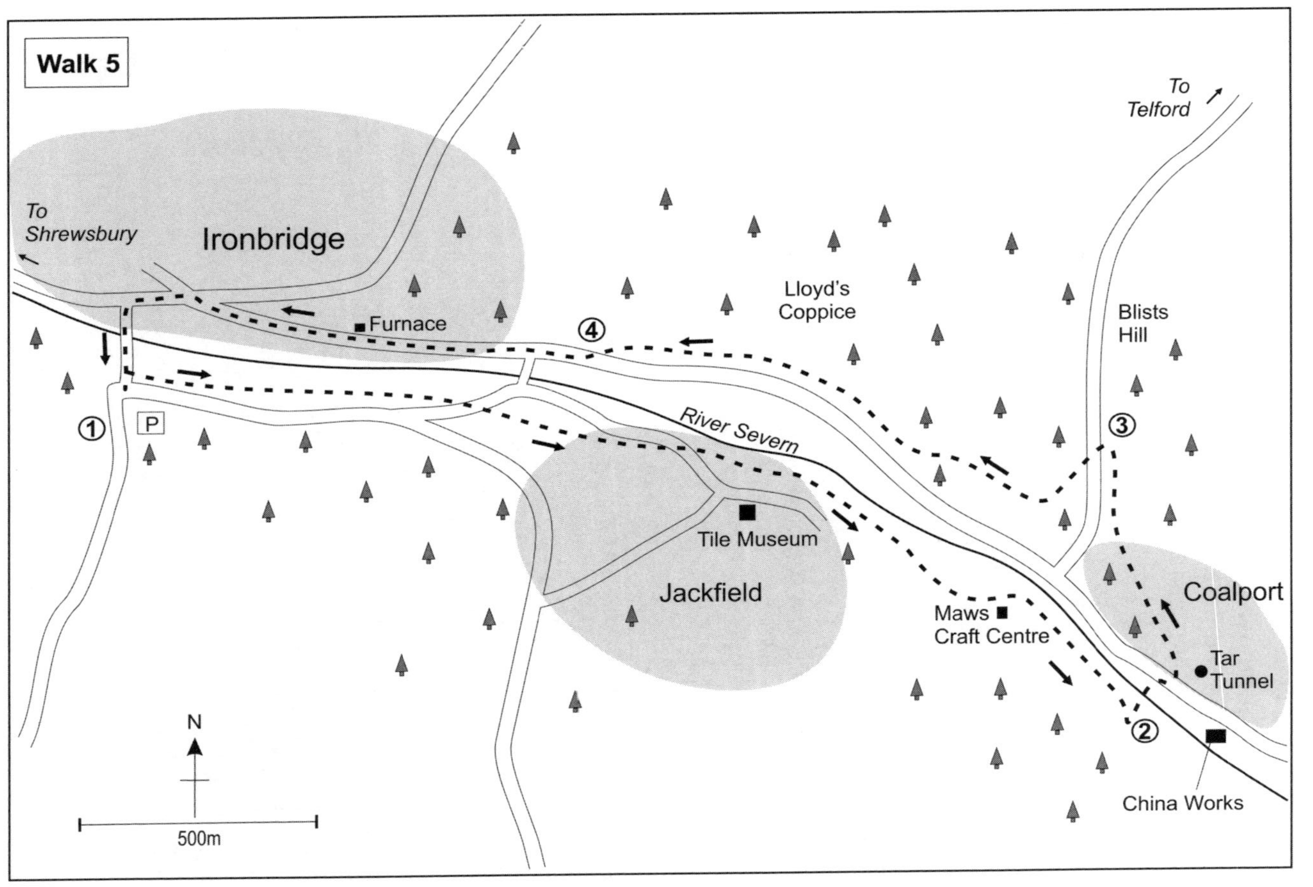

Walk 5
To Telford
To Shrewsbury
Ironbridge
Furnace
Lloyd's Coppice
Blists Hill
River Severn
Tile Museum
Jackfield
Maws Craft Centre
Coalport
Tar Tunnel
China Works
P
N
500m

a path at the corner of the buildings, continue along it and after the end of the buildings, keep ahead along Ferry Road, passing in front of cottages to the Boat Inn.

2. Opposite the pub, turn left to cross a footbridge over the river into Coalport, climb steps up to a road and turn right. The Coalport China Museum is a short distance ahead.

Coalport China is renowned throughout the world and the museum attracts many visitors. It contains collections of Coalport China, plus displays and demonstrations on the history and techniques of china production.

On the left is the bottom of the Hay Inclined Plane. Boats were transported between the canal at Blist Hill at the top of the incline and the Coalport Canal and River Severn here at the bottom. They were hauled by rope and the descending boats counter balanced those that were being pulled up. It is now part of the Blists Hill Victorian town.

Just beyond the Shakespeare Inn, turn left, at a public footpath sign Silkin Way, and follow a path around a series of hairpin bends up to a T-junction. Turn left, in the Madeley and Victorian Town direction, and the track passes through a tunnel under the Hay Incline. Keep ahead along the pleasant wooded track which later runs parallel to a road on the left. Just after going through a long tunnel, look out for some steps to the right. Go up them, turn right and turn right again to the road. Part of the Blists Hill Museum can be seen ahead when you leave the track. The entrance is more than ½ mile (0.8 km) along the main road and there is so much to see and do there that it might be better to visit it separately. Blists Hill is a recreation of a typical Victorian industrial town, with buildings brought and relocated here from other parts of the Midlands. There are shops, cottages and various workplaces of the era and visitors can ride on a horse and cart and enjoy a Victorian fairground.

3. Cross the road, turn left and almost immediately, at a footpath sign 'Ironbridge via Wood', turn right along a track in front of a row of cottages. Turn right up steps to another footpath sign and turn left,

again following directions to Ironbridge, to a kissing gate. Go through, head uphill along a narrow path to a crossways and keep ahead along a winding path through the lovely woodland of Lloyds Coppice, now heading downhill and descending several flights of steps. On reaching a T-junction at the bottom of a particularly long flight, turn right along a track. At a fork, take the right hand path, signposted to Ironbridge, and this winding and undulating path eventually descends to a kissing gate. Go through and keep ahead to a road.

4. Turn right and follow it for just over ½ mile (0.8 km) back to Ironbridge, passing the Bedlam Furnaces. These were built in the 1750s and were amongst the earliest furnaces to use the new technique of using coke in the smelting of iron ore. Finally turn left over the Iron Bridge to return to the car park.

River Severn near Ironbridge

6. Shifnal and Kemberton

'An antique, interesting village'

Distance	6 ½ miles (10.5 km)
Approximate time	3 ½ hours
Start	Shifnal, bottom end of the main street (Bradford Street) near the railway bridge, grid ref SJ749077
Parking	Shifnal
Terrain	Easy walking on well-waymarked paths and tracks across gentle slopes, over fields and through woods
Refreshments	Pubs and cafes at Shifnal, pub at Kemberton
Public Transport	Buses from Shrewsbury, Telford, Bridgnorth and Wolverhampton; trains from Birmingham, Wolverhampton and Shrewsbury
Map	OS Explorer 242 (Telford, Ironbridge and The Wrekin)

Elihu Burritt and his walking companion Edward Capern came to Shifnal because they used it as the starting point for a long walk that took in Tong, Boscobel House and Brewood, finishing at Spread Eagle station from where they returned to Birmingham. Incidentally this station was renamed Gailey in 1881 after the nearest village and closed in 1951, although the line still runs through the site. This walk does not follow that route as much of it is now along roads but instead explores the highly attractive, undulating countryside to the south and west of Shifnal between the town and the village of Kemberton. Throughout most of the route there are fine and extensive views over the surrounding countryside.

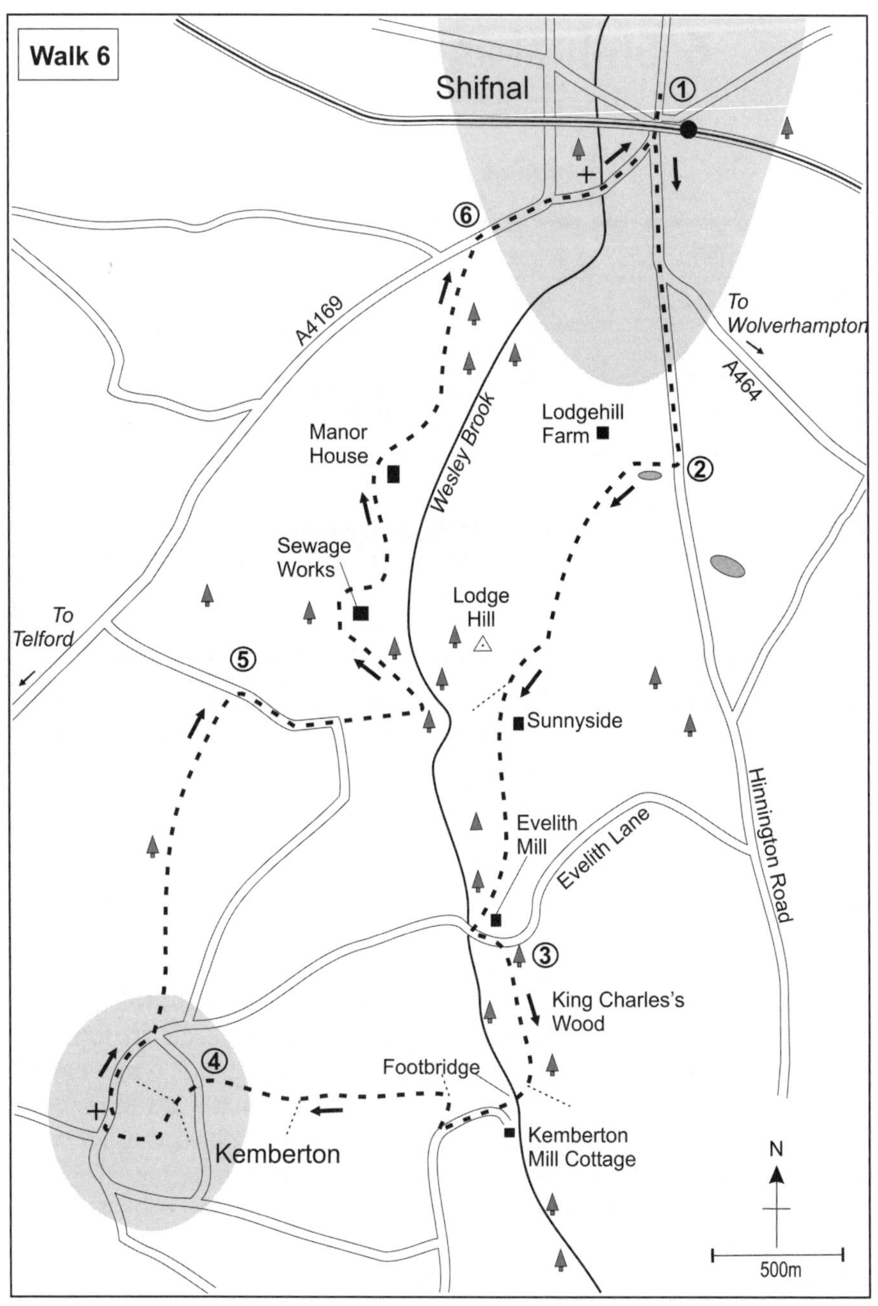

Walk 6
Shifnal
①
To Wolverhampton
A464
②
A4169
Wesley Brook
Manor House
Lodgehill Farm
Lodge Hill
Sewage Works
To Telford
⑤
Sunnyside
Evelith Mill
Evelith Lane
Hinnington Road
③
King Charles's Wood
④
Footbridge
Kemberton
Kemberton Mill Cottage
⑥
N
500m

The Walk

1. Begin by walking along Bradford Street towards the railway bridge. Pass under it, keep ahead and where the road bends left, bear right along Park Lane.

2. After nearly ½ mile (0.8 km) and just before a speed derestriction sign, turn right, at a public footpath sign, along an enclosed track to a stile. Climb it and walk along a path, between a pool on the left and a hedge on the right. The path curves left, now with a hedge on the left and a fence on the right, curves slightly to the left again and continues as an enclosed path to a stile. Climb it and head gently uphill over the slopes of Lodge Hill which, although only reaching the modest height of 374 feet (114m), gives superb views over the surrounding countryside, including the houses and church tower of Kemberton ahead. On the brow of the hill – there is a circular clump of trees in the field on the right – bear left and head downhill in the direction of farm buildings, making for a stile. After climbing it, walk along the track ahead and just after passing a bungalow on the right, look out for a public footpath sign where you turn right over a stile. Bear right across a field to climb another stile which admits you to woodland and continue along a path that keeps by the left inside edge of the trees before descending gently to a stile. Climb it, continue through the wood and turn right in front of a brick building. At a T-junction, turn left along a drive and go through a gate onto a lane. Turn left, passing in front of a former mill building.

3. At a public bridleway sign, turn right onto a track through King Charles's Wood. On reaching a T-junction and fingerpost, turn right to cross a footbridge over a stream and the path curves left, crossing another footbridge. Keep ahead by a wall corner to a T-junction and turn right along a track, in the Kemberton direction. Immediately after going through a gate, turn sharp right to a fingerpost and continue along a hedge-lined path to a gate. Turn left over a stile in front of the gate, keep along the left edge of a field and after about 50 yards (46m) – by a tree on the right with a waymark fixed to it – turn left onto a clear, wide, grassy path which heads uphill between fields. Keep ahead

to a T-junction on the far side, turn right along a track and in the field corner turn left onto a path by the right field edge. Pass through a fence gap and continue along a hedge-lined path to a lane.

4. Turn left, turn right at a public footpath sign along a track to the right of a house and continue along the right edge of a field. Ignore the first waymarked post on the right, keep ahead and just after emerging onto a gravel track opposite a house, turn right up steps and go through a kissing gate. Head diagonally uphill across a field, making for a kissing gate in the top left hand corner. After going through it, turn right along a grassy track and go through a gate onto a road in Kemberton.

The tower of Kemberton church has already been visible during parts of the walk. Although of a medieval appearance and occupying an ancient site, this fine looking sandstone church only dates from a rebuilding in the 1880s.

Kemberton church

Turn right, passing the church, and where the road bends right, turn left, at a public footpath sign, along an enclosed track to a gate. Go through it, keep ahead over two stiles in quick succession and continue across a field. On the far side follow a winding path down through a belt of trees to enter the next field. Turn right along the right edge of two fields – this is on a permissive path – and go through a gate onto a lane.

5. Turn right and where the lane becomes a rough track, keep ahead downhill into woodland. At a fork, take the left hand track which bends left and continues through the wooded valley. Just before reaching the gates to a sewage works, bear left uphill along a path and go up steps onto a track. Cross it and bear left onto an enclosed path which curves right above a wooded dell. Follow the fence of the sewage works on the right, bending left and heading down to a kissing gate. Go through, head gently uphill along an enclosed path, turn left through a gate and keep ahead. Follow the path around three right hand bends to reach a kissing gate and turn left along a broad track. Follow it for about ¾ mile (1.2 km) to a road.

6. Turn right into Shifnal and at a junction, keep ahead along Church Street to the church.

Burritt enthused over Shifnal's sturdy-looking cruciform church, describing it as a 'massive old church, evidently the growth of centuries'. He adds 'it is an impressive old building, wearing its venerable antiquity with hardly a court plaster of modern improvements to cover a wrinkle'. Most of those observations still hold true today and there is not much to add to them apart from stating

The impressive medieval church at Shifnal

that the church dates mainly from the 13th and 14th centuries and retains a Norman chancel arch from an earlier building.

Continue along Church Street to a T-junction, turn left and go under the railway bridge to return to the start.

Rolling countryside between Shifnal anf Kemberton

7. Tong

'It is doubtful if any other village or provincial church in England contains within its walls so many beautiful and costly monuments to the memory of so many noble families as this little Westminster'

Distance	3 ½ miles (5.6 km)
Approximate time	2 hours
Start	Tong, just to the east of the A41 between Newport and Wolverhampton, grid ref SJ796074
Parking	Roadside parking by the church
Terrain	Flat and easy walking along clear tracks
Refreshments	None
Public Transport	Buses from Telford and Wolverhampton
Map	OS Explorer 242 (Telford, Ironbridge and The Wrekin)

The busy A41 lies to the west and the even busier M54 is a short distance to the south, obliterating the site of the former castle, but Tong is still a pleasant village with some attractive old black and white cottages. Elihu Burritt was passing through here on his walk from Shifnal to Boscobel House and spent a night at the Bell Inn just up the A41 at Tong Norton but what particularly attracted his admiration and enthusiasm was the fine collegiate church. The walk is a short, pleasant and easy route to the east of the village.

The Walk

The church at Tong is an unusually imposing one for a small village because it was a collegiate church, a church served by a college or community of priests, founded in 1410. Elihu Burritt referred to it as a ' village Westminster Abbey' and 'this miniature cathedral, for such it is and

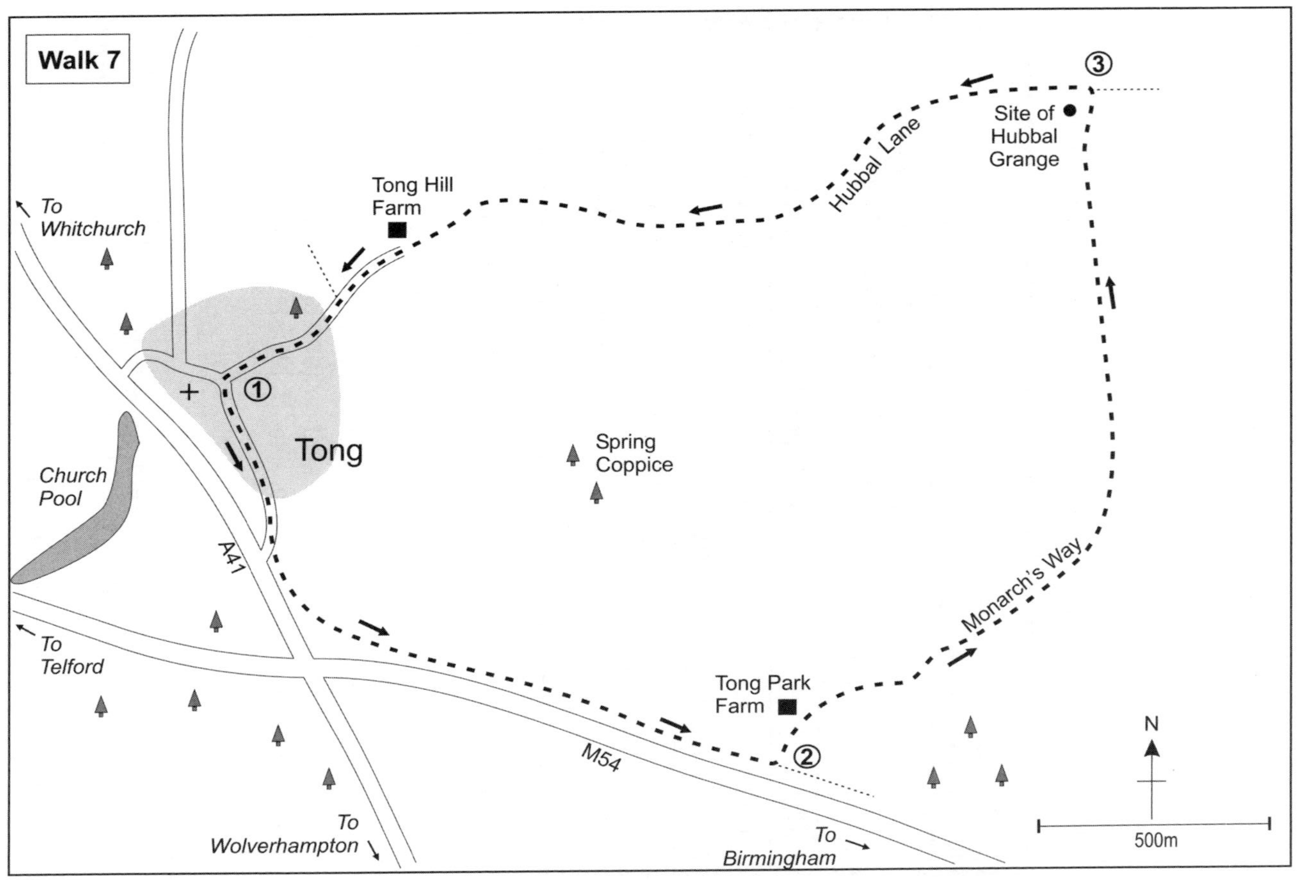

Walk 7
To Whitchurch
Hubbal Lane
Site of Hubbal Grange
Tong Hill Farm
Tong
Church Pool
Spring Coppice
Monarch's Way
To Telford
A41
M54
Tong Park Farm
To Wolverhampton
To Birmingham
N
500m

Tong church, Elihu Burritt's 'village Westminster Abbey'

looks in its interior and exterior aspects' on account of its size and grandeur, its cruciform shape but principally because of its large number of monuments. These are of the Pembrugges, Vernons and Stanleys, the various prominent local families who resided in the now vanished Tong Castle and who dominated this area over the centuries. Apart from the many monuments, look out for the fan vaulting in the Golden Chapel, something usually only seen in the grander cathedrals and abbeys or at some of the Oxford and Cambridge colleges. Burritt acknowledges its significance by describing it as 'the Henry VII's Chapel of this little Westminster'. Externally the church's most impressive feature is the partly octagonal central tower, topped by a short spire, seen at its best from the large churchyard.

1. Facing the church, turn left along the road and where it bends right to the A41, bear left along a concrete track which runs parallel to the M54 motorway, the latter out of sight if not out of hearing. Later it becomes

Old houses in Tong village

a rough track and where it bears left, keep ahead, at a waymarked post, along a grassy track, still parallel to the motorway.

2. At a T-junction, turn left along a concrete track, passing in front of a farm, and at a Monarchs Way sign, turn right along a fence-lined track to a gate. Go through, turn left to another gate, go through that and continue along a track, which later narrows to a path, keeping along the left field edge. In the corner of the field turn right to a gate and after going through, keep in a roughly straight line – first along a right field edge, then an enclosed track and finally along a left field edge – to reach a T-junction and fingerpost.

There is nothing left to see but at this corner previously stood Hubbal Grange, home of one of the Penderel brothers who assisted Charles II when he was on the run from Cromwell's soldiers following his defeat at the Battle of Worcester in September 1651. It is one of a number of places in the vicinity that gave food and shelter to the fugitive king.

3. Turn left onto an attractive, hedge-and tree-lined track from which there are fine views of The Wrekin. The track eventually becomes a tarmac lane which leads back into Tong opposite the church.

View of The Wrekin near Tong

8. Boscobel House and White Ladies Priory

'That house so celebrated in English history and so vitally connected with the life and death crisis in the experience of Charles II'

Distance	4 ½ miles (7.2 km)
Approximate time	2 hours
Start	Boscobel House, on minor road ½ mile (0.8 km) south of Bishops Wood, grid ref SJ837084
Parking	English Heritage car park at Boscobel House, if house is closed park carefully at the side of the lane
Terrain	Flat and easy walking along roads, tracks and field paths
Refreshments	None
Public Transport	None
Map	OS Explorer 242 (Telford, Ironbridge and The Wrekin)

Elihu Burritt took a keen interest in and had an almost boyish enthusiasm for everywhere he visited and none more so than Boscobel House. This was because of its associations with Charles II's escape from Cromwell's soldiers, which included hiding from them in a nearby oak tree, while a fugitive in September 1651. He described the house as 'the chief point of interest we had in view when we left home' and gives a detailed and lengthy description of the events surrounding the king's stay at both Boscobel House and the nearby White Ladies Priory. This pleasant and easy walk starts at the house, passes White Ladies Priory and enables you to view the oak tree – or rather its successor – in which the king hid from his pursuers.

The Walk

Boscobel House is a fine but modest example of a 17th century timber-framed house but what makes it particularly fascinating is its pivotal role in one of the major events of the Civil War era. After his devastating defeat at the hands of Cromwell's army at the Battle of Worcester on 3rd September 1651, Charles II was forced to go on the run to escape capture and possible execution. His initial intention was to make for Scotland and he headed northwards, seeking refuge in the homes of known Royalist sympathisers. At both the houses in which he stayed in this area – Boscobel and White Ladies – he was looked after by four brothers, the Penderels. His first night was spent at White Ladies Priory but because the area was swarming with Cromwell's soldiers the king was forced to hide for a while in a nearby wood, Spring Coppice, which is still marked on the Ordnance Survey map. Charles then decided to change his plans and head for Wales, a Royalist stronghold, but the crossing of the River Severn was so closely guarded that he was forced to abandon that idea. He retraced his steps to

Boscobel House

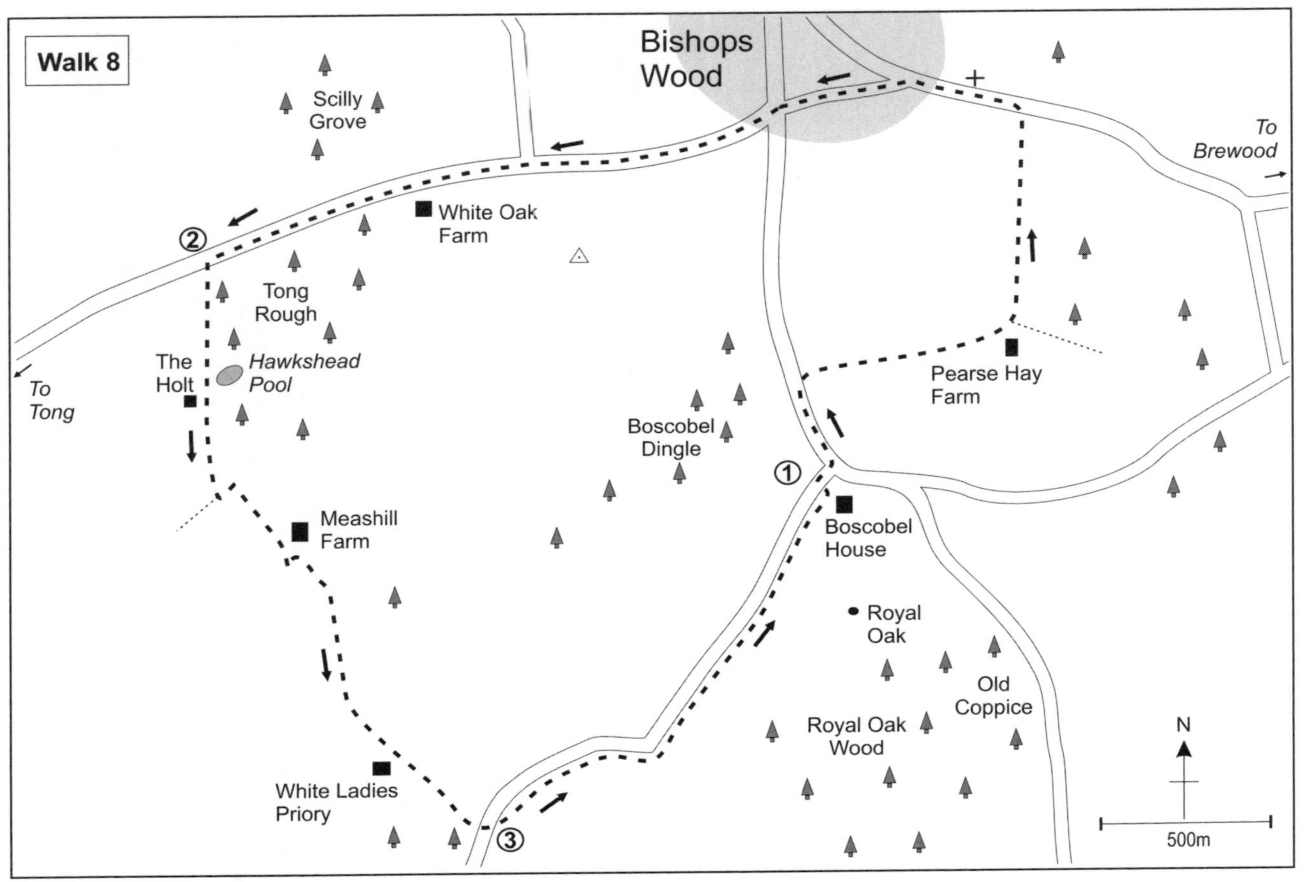
Walk 8
Bishops Wood
Scilly Grove
White Oak Farm
Tong Rough
The Holt
Hawkshead Pool
To Tong
Boscobel Dingle
Pearse Hay Farm
To Brewood
Meashill Farm
Boscobel House
Royal Oak
Old Coppice
White Ladies Priory
Royal Oak Wood
N
500m

Boscobel House but again, because of the presence of so many of Cromwell's soldiers, it was considered unsafe to stay in the house itself and instead he spent a rather uncomfortable day (6th September) hiding in a nearby oak tree. He came down from the tree after dark and spent a rather more pleasant night in the house, finally leaving on the evening of the next day.

Not surprisingly the house has priest's holes (Charles hid in one of these) and there are attractive gardens. From the grounds a path leads from the house to the Royal Oak. The original tree was destroyed in the 17th and 18th centuries by over-zealous souvenir hunters and the present tree is a descendant. It is in a rather sorry state at the present time, certainly not capable of giving shelter to anyone, as a result of severe storm damage in 2000 followed by the appearance of several serious cracks in 2010. Currently it is protected by a perimeter fence and has supporting bands around the trunk. Nearby a daughter tree is growing beside it.

The successor to the Royal Oak at Boscobel

1. Turn right out of the car park along the lane to a T-junction and turn left. At a public footpath sign, turn right along an enclosed track, part of the Monarchs Way, and just after passing some barns on the right, turn left along another hedge-lined track. Follow it to a road and turn left, passing Bishops Wood's Victorian church. At a fork, take the left hand road, signposted to Tong and Codsall, and keep along it for about 1 mile (1.6 km).

2. At the corner of a wood (Tong Rough), turn left along a hedge-lined tarmac track. This track has a sign Private Road but underneath is a

waymark indicating a public right of way. After just under ½ mile (0.8 km), follow the track around first a left and then a right bend to reach a farm. At a public footpath sign in front of the farmhouse turn left to a gate, bear right across the farmyard and in the far corner, turn sharp right. Turn left around the corner of buildings and continue along an enclosed path. At this point there are fine views all around, with The Wrekin prominent in the distance on the right. The path later heads gently downhill and continues as a tree-lined path to the remains of White Ladies Priory, accessed via a kissing gate on the right.

In the Middle Ages White Ladies Priory was a small, poor and remote nunnery but after the closure of the monasteries in the 1530s, a large house was built on the site. This was the building which gave shelter to Charles II in 1651 but it has now entirely disappeared, revealing once more the sparse but picturesque 12th century ruins of the original nunnery.

From the priory, continue along the path to go through a gate onto a lane and turn left.

The sparse remains of White Ladies Priory

3. Here there is a choice. Either follow the lane back to Boscobel House, or turn right through a gate, at a Permissive Access notice, and walk along a series of field edges parallel to the lane. The advantage of using the path is that as you approach the house, there are fine views both of the house and the Royal Oak.

9. Brewood and the Shropshire Union Canal

'That snug little town'

Distance	5 miles (8 km)
Approximate time	2 ½ hours
Start	Brewood, Market Place, grid ref SJ884088
Parking	Brewood
Terrain	Easy walking along tracks, field paths and a canal towpath
Refreshments	Pubs and café at Brewood
Public Transport	Buses from Wolverhampton and Stafford
Map	OS Explorer 242 (Telford, Ironbridge & The Wrekin)

Brewood was a brief stopping place on the last stage of Elhu Burritt's walk from Shifnal to Gailey but he was impressed with the town, especially – as at Shifnal and Tong – with the fine church. From the town centre, the route explores the pleasant, undulating countryside to the south of the town, returning via the towpath of the Shropshire Union Canal.

The Walk

In the Middle Ages Brewood was at the centre of a forest, one of a number of royal forests in

The church at Brewood, Elihu Burritt's 'large church in that snug little town'

Staffordshire at the time. Elihu Burritt's description of it as 'that snug little town' still holds true today, with streets lined by pleasant old houses and cottages radiating from the Market Place. The most unusual building in the town centre is 'Speedwell Castle', an 18th century Gothic folly built by a local eccentric reputedly from his horse racing winnings. The most impressive is undoubtedly the church, built mainly in the 13th century with a 15th century tower and spire, although much altered in later restorations. Inside are tombs of the Giffard family, who lived at nearby Chillington Hall.

1. Start in the Market Place and with your back to the Lion Hotel, walk down the road towards the church. At a T-junction by the church, turn left and almost immediately turn right, at a public footpath sign, along an enclosed path. The path bends first to the right and then to the left to emerge onto a track. Turn left, turn right through a kissing gate, at a public footpath sign, and head gently downhill along the left field

Brewood from the canal

Walk 9
To Bishops Wood
Brewood
①
Dean's Hall Bridge
②
The Woolley
Hyde Farm
Avenue Bridge
Horse Paddock Wood
Park Lane
Shropshire Union Canal
Upper Avenue
③
Chillington Hall
Chillington Street
Long Birch Farm
Hunting Bridge
④
N
500m
To Wolverhampton

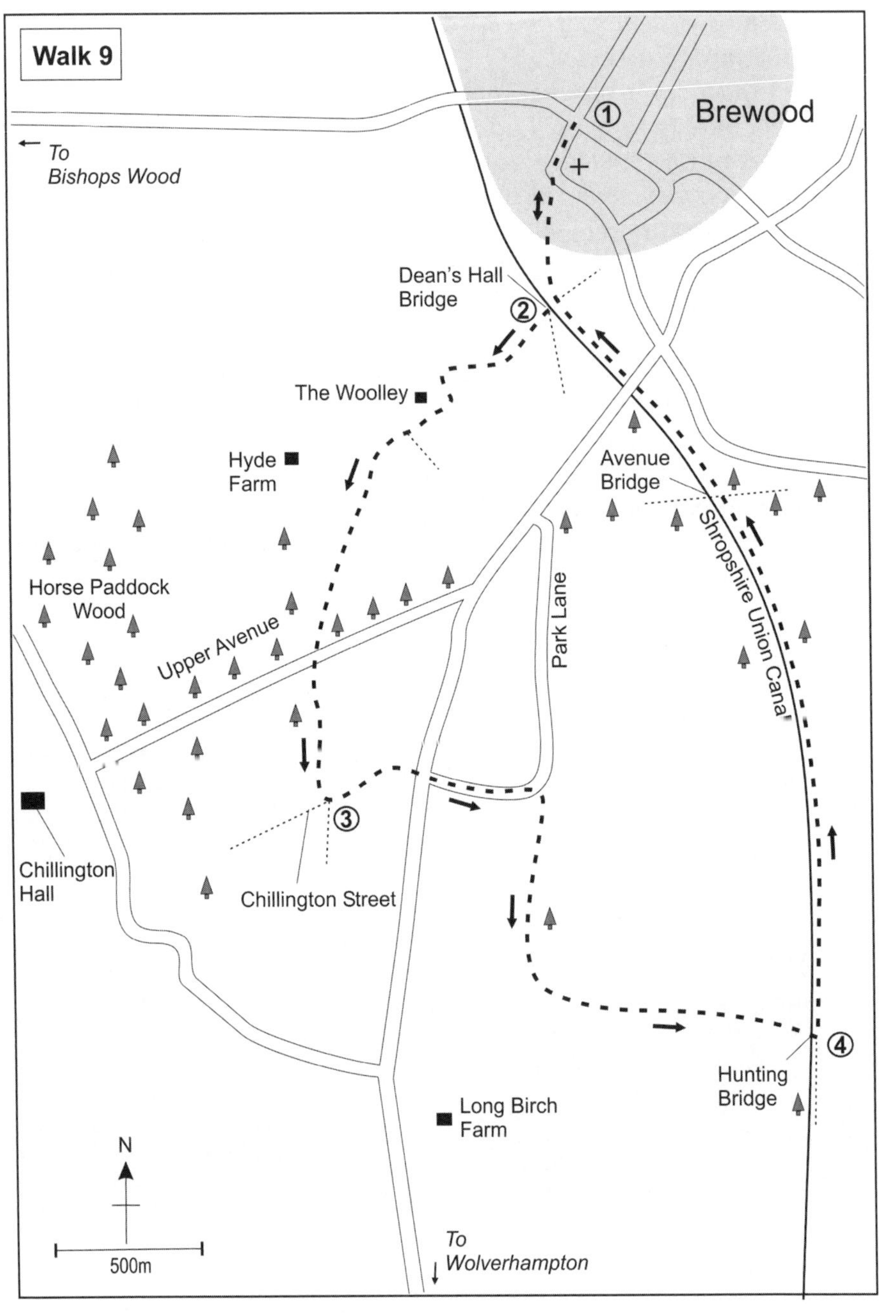

58

edge. After going through three more kissing gates you reach the towpath of the Shropshire Union Canal.

2. Do not continue along it but ascend the steps in front, climb a stile and turn right to cross the canal bridge. Continue along an enclosed track and after ¼ mile (0.4 km), look out for where a Staffordshire Way sign directs you to turn left onto another enclosed track. Keep ahead at a crossways and just after a left bend, there is a kissing gate on the left with a Staffordshire Way sign. Go through it and walk along the left edge of a field, by an old hedgeline on the left. In the corner go through a kissing gate, keep ahead to go through another one and continue across a wide, grassy drive. To the right is a fine view of the façade of Chillington Hall.

This elegant Classical country house, home of the Giffards, was built in the 1720s and enlarged later in the 18th century. The parkland was landscaped by 'Capability' Brown and the grassy drive, part of the Upper and Lower Avenues, was designed to make an impressive approach to the house.

Façade of Chillington Hall

3. Pass through a belt of trees on the far side and go through a kissing gate onto a lane. Cross over, go through the kissing gate opposite and walk along the left edge of a large field.

After going through a kissing gate in the corner, turn left along an enclosed track (Chillington Street) which emerges onto a road. Cross over, take the narrow lane opposite and where it bends sharply to the left, turn right along an enclosed track. After nearly ½ mile (0.8 km), look out for where a public bridleway sign for the Monarchs Way on the right of the track directs you to turn left along the right edge of a field. Just before reaching the field corner, bear right through a hedge gap, bear left through a line of trees and continue along the left edge of the next field.

4. In the corner keep ahead to cross a canal bridge, turn sharp right down to the towpath and right again to pass under the bridge.

The Shropshire Union Canal was built by the renowned engineer Thomas Telford and completed in 1834. It links the canal system of Birmingham and the Black Country with Shropshire, Cheshire and the River Mersey. Look out for the impressive Avenue Bridge, built by Telford in the Classical style to harmonise with the hall and parkland at Chillington. Even so the Giffards insisted that the canal ran through a deep cutting here so that it could not be seen from the house.

Keep along the towpath for 1 ½ miles (2.4 km) and just after passing under bridge number 12, turn right through a kissing gate. Here you rejoin the outward route and retrace your steps to the start.

Avenue Bridge, on the Shropshire Union Canal

10. Around Lichfield

'Looks like a city of steeples on approaching it in any direction'

Distance	2 ¾ miles (4.4 km)
Approximate time	1 ½ hours
Start	Lichfield, Market Square, grid ref SK117096
Parking	Lichfield
Terrain	Easy walking mostly on tarmac paths
Refreshments	Pubs and cafes at Lichfield, café in Beacon Park
Public Transport	Buses and trains from Birmingham, Tamworth, Stafford and all the surrounding towns
Map	OS Explorers 232 (Nuneaton & Tamworth) and 244 (Cannock Chase & Chasewater)

Elihu Burritt's observation about Lichfield looking like 'a city of steeples' still holds true today because both as you approach and later walk around this small and attractive cathedral city, most of the views are dominated by the triple spires of the medieval cathedral. This pleasant walk does a figure of eight around the city, with the cathedral at the focal point. The first loop is around Beacon Park to the west of the cathedral and the second is a circuit of Stowe Pool to the east of it, passing the ancient St Chad's church.

The Walk

The Market Square is dominated by the large 19th century church of St Mary, now the Lichfield Heritage Centre. In one corner of the square is Dr Johnson's House, a museum to Lichfield's most famous son who was born here in 1709. Elihu Burritt was obviously a great admirer of Johnson as he writes: 'a nation that could build fifty cathedrals in ten years would need

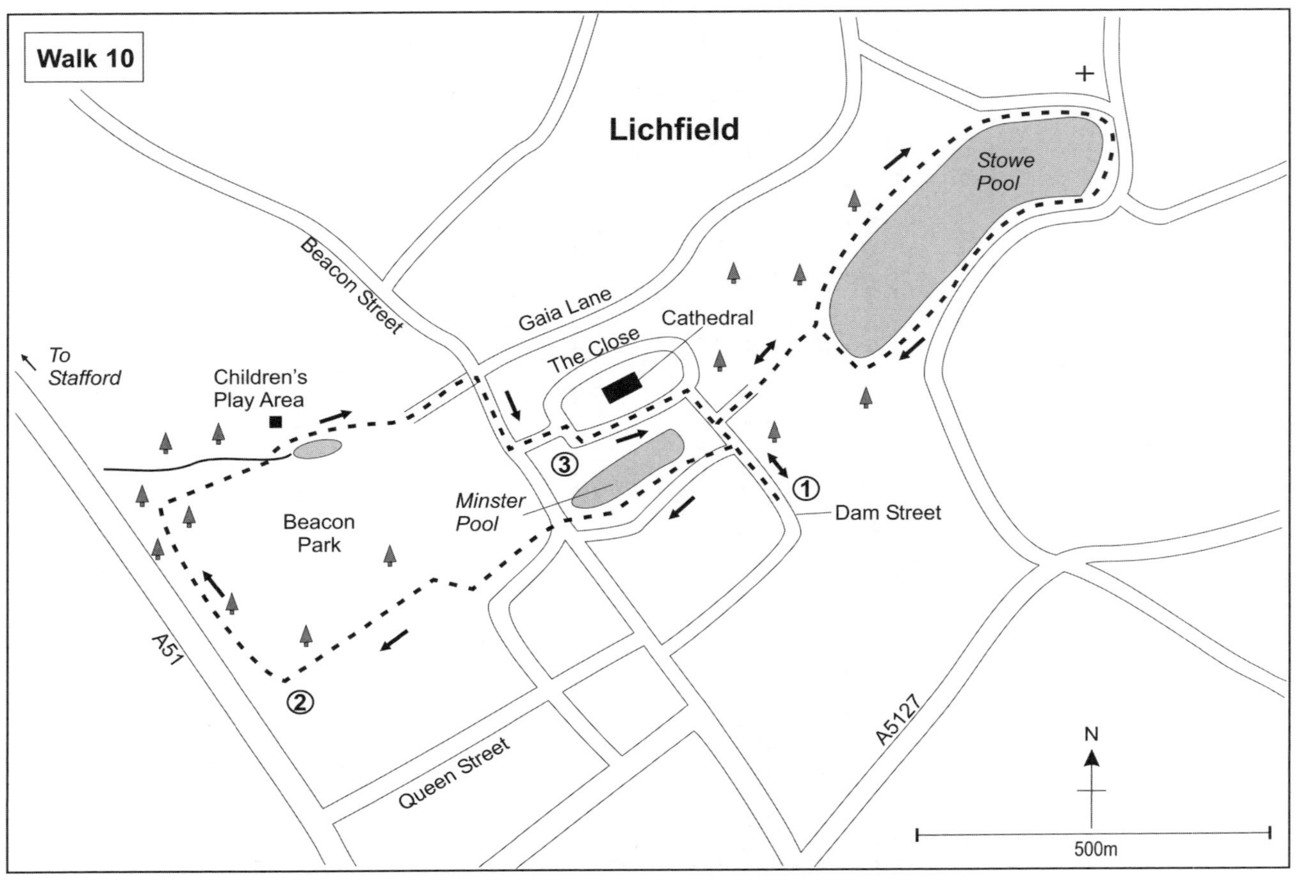

Walk 10
Lichfield
Stowe Pool
Beacon Street
Gaia Lane
The Close
Cathedral
To Stafford
Children's Play Area
Minster Pool
Beacon Park
Dam Street
Queen Street
A51
A5127
N
500m
1
2
3

a century for building such another man as he was to the world of mind and thought.'

1. Begin by walking along Dam Street towards the cathedral and take the first turning on the left (Pool Walk). This path keeps by the left edge of Minster Pool to emerge onto a road. Burritt describes Minster Pool as 'a long, wide pool of water, almost a lake, which serves as a mirror in which you see the three spires and the upper part of the grand edifice photographed as large and true as life'. Cross over and take the path opposite (to the right of a toilet block) to enter Beacon Park. At a fork immediately ahead, continue along the left hand path by the left edge of the park. Bear first right and then left – there are tennis courts to the right, curving right again to join another path. At a crossways turn left onto a broad path, in the direction of a footpath sign NCR5, continue across the park, by the left edge of playing fields, and pass beside a barrier into a car park.

The magnificent west front of Lichfield Cathedral

2. At the far end of the car park turn right onto a path which soon enters trees and keep along it, parallel to the A51 over to the left, to a footbridge over a stream. Just before reaching the bridge, turn sharp right along a path through trees – there is a golf course to the left. The path emerges from the trees and continues along the left edge of a

The three spires of the cathedral reflected in the pool in Beacon Park

playing field, with a view of the cathedral spires ahead. Turn left to cross a zigzag footbridge over the stream and turn right along a path beside a children's play area on the left. At a T-junction turn left to exit the park, pass through a car park and at a Heart of England waymark, keep ahead along a lane to a road. Turn right, turn left into The Close and walk up to the west front of the cathedral.

Burritt described Lichfield Cathedral as 'an edifice of which a whole nation might be proud' and went on to declare that 'having visited all the cathedrals of Great Britain and studied them with all the interest of American admiration for such structures, I am inclined to believe that this exceeds all others in the quality of beauty, both in its exterior and interior structure and embellishment'. It is certainly one of the finest medieval cathedrals in the country, the only one with three spires, and the views of the triple spires rising above Minster Pool are especially memorable. The cathedral was founded in 669 by St Chad and the present church was built mainly between the late 12th and early 14th centuries. It suffered much damage during the Civil War and has needed several major restorations but is a superb example of Gothic architecture, particularly noted for the ornate west front.

3. Keep to the right along the south side of the cathedral and turn right at the far end. Take the first turning on the left (Reeve Lane) and continue along a hedge-lined path which later keeps along the left edge of Stowe Pool. The next part of the walk is a circuit of the pool.

At the far end of the pool you pass St Chad's church. This ancient structure was originally founded in the 7th century by St Chad, first bishop of Lichfield, but the present building dates mainly from the 13th century. During the Civil War it was used as a storehouse for munitions and suffered extensive damage. In the subsequent restoration the upper part of the nave was rebuilt in brick.

On completing the circuit, retrace your steps along Reeve Lane to Dam Street and turn left along it to return to the Market Square.

Stowe Pool and St Chad's Church

11. Kenilworth: Castle and Abbey Ruins

'For its historical associations as well as for its architectural character disclosed in its picturesque ruins, Kenilworth, perhaps stands at the head of all old English castles'

Distance	3 ½ miles (5.6 km)
Approximate time	2 hours
Start	Kenilworth, vehicle entrance to Abbey Fields, grid ref SP287725
Parking	Kenilworth, Abbey Fields car park
Terrain	Parkland and fields
Refreshments	Pubs and cafes at Kenilworth
Public Transport	Buses from Coventry, Leamington and Warwick
Map	OS Explorer 221 (Coventry & Warwick)

Although short, this is a walk full of interest. It is a figure of eight walk, with the castle at the fulcrum of the figure and starts in the attractive Abbey Fields, now a park but formerly the land surrounding Kenilworth Abbey. Of this once wealthy institution hardly anything remains but of Kenilworth's mighty castle there are fortunately substantial remains of buildings dating from the 12th to 16th centuries, plus a reconstruction of the Tudor garden. From many points on the walk there are superb views of the castle, particularly from the path that skirts its outer walls and the return path that takes you across a series of fields.

The Walk

1. Begin by passing beside a barrier and walking along the straight, tree-lined tarmac path across the park to the swimming pool complex. Turn left at the end of the buildings, do not cross the footbridge over a

stream but turn right and continue between the stream on the left and Abbey Pool on the right to emerge onto a road.

2. Turn left, curving right uphill, and turn right into the Castle car park.

Elihu Burritt visited Kenilworth on a bright autumn day and was most impressed with the castle, although he seems to have preferred churches. Despite his favourable quotation that follows the heading of this walk, he goes on to comment that 'on walking around these broken walls...one must be struck with the weak vitality they possess compared with the religious buildings of the country, which seemingly renovate themselves into perpetual strength and beauty.' Few of today's visitors would agree with him on that.

It is certainly one of the most impressive and formidable medieval castles in the country and at its height it was surrounded by extensive water defences to make up for its situation on low lying ground. The

Kenilworth's mighty castle

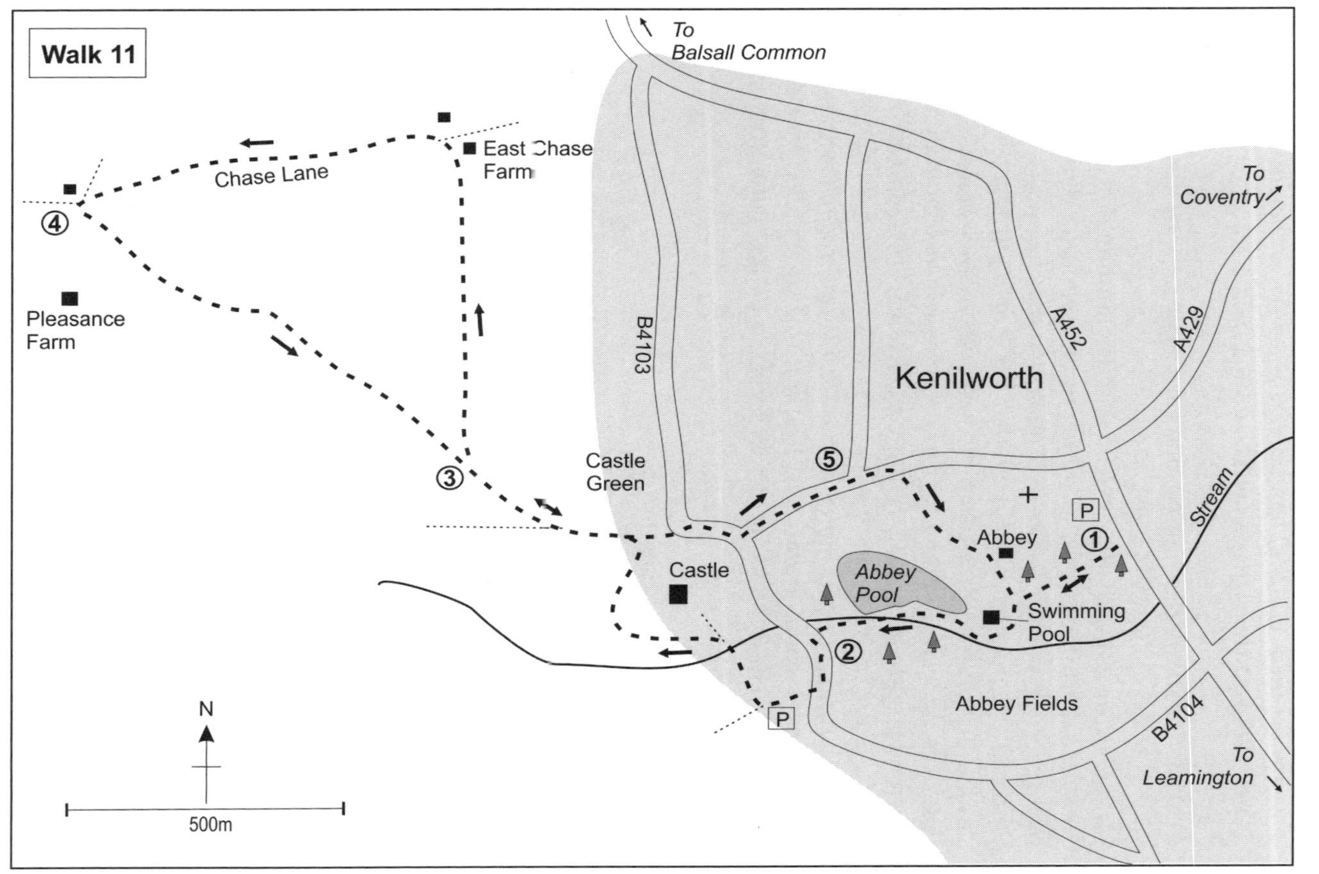

Walk 11
To Balsall Common
Chase Lane
East Chase Farm
Pleasance Farm
Castle Green
B4103
Kenilworth
A452
A429
Stream
To Coventry
Abbey
P
Abbey Pool
Castle
Swimming Pool
Abbey Fields
B4104
To Leamington
N
500m

castle was founded by Geoffrey de Clinton in the 12th century and throughout its long history it has had a variety of powerful owners, both baronial and royal. These include Simon de Montfort (leader of a barons' revolt against Henry III in the 13th century), John of Gaunt (son of Edward III) and Robert Dudley, Earl of Leicester and favourite of Elizabeth I. Perhaps the most momentous event in its history, told in detail by Burritt,

The monastic barn and abbey gatehouse are all that remain of Kenilworth's medieval abbey

is the lavish entertainment provided by Dudley on the visit of Elizabeth in 1575. The most impressive remains are the great 12th century keep, John of Gaunt's magnificent 14th century banqueting hall and Robert Dudley's 16th century gatehouse and barn. A major attraction for many visitors is the Tudor garden which has been recently restored.

Just beyond the path that leads across a bridge to the castle entrance, bear right down to a T-junction and turn right onto a path that keeps below the castle walls. Go through a kissing gate, continue below the castle walls and where the walls turn right, keep ahead across grass and go through a gate onto a track. Turn left and at a public footpath sign to Chase Lane, turn right through a kissing gate and take the gently ascending path across a field to a public footpath sign on the far side.

3. At a fork just beyond the sign, continue along the right hand path across a field, later keeping along its right edge to a kissing gate in the corner. Go through, keep ahead towards farm buildings, bearing left away from the field edge towards a fence corner and continue past it to a stile. Climb it and turn left along a tarmac track (Chase Lane).

4. On reaching houses, turn left through a kissing gate, at a public footpath sign to Purlieu Lane, and head diagonally across a field. Go

through a kissing gate on the far side, turn left along the edge of the next field, go through a kissing gate and pass through a small group of trees into the next field. Continue across it and from now on come a succession of superb views of the castle. Go through another kissing gate, continue across the next field and on the far side, you rejoin the previous route. (3) Retrace your steps back to the castle but instead of turning right below the castle walls, continue along the track up to the road at Castle Green. Keep ahead and where the main road bends right, bear left up Castle Hill.

Old cottages on Castle Green at Kenilworth

5. On the brow of the hill – where Castle Hill becomes High Street – turn right through a gap to re-enter Abbey Fields and follow a winding path gently downhill, passing the scanty remains of the abbey.

Abbey gatehouse at Kenilworth

Like the castle, Kenilworth Abbey was founded in the 12th century by Geoffrey de Clinton. It was originally a priory but was later upgraded to an abbey. Unlike the castle little remains – just the vaulted gatehouse and barn. Nearby is the medieval church. Perhaps surprisingly for someone particularly interested in churches, Elihu Burritt mentions neither abbey remains nor church.

Continue down to the swimming pool buildings and turn left to retrace your steps the short distance to the start.

12. Ashow and Stoneleigh Abbey

'The landscape of the park is truly beautiful'

Distance	3 ½ miles (5.6 km)
Approximate time	2 hours
Start	Ashow, bottom end of the lane through the village, grid ref SP313703
Parking	There is limited parking at the end of the lane through the village near the village hall, otherwise park considerately beside the lane or on verges outside the village
Terrain	Flat walking along lanes, a drive and woodland paths
Refreshments	Tearoom at Stoneleigh Abbey
Public Transport	None
Map	OS Explorer 221 (Coventry & Warwick)

Elihu Burritt and Edward Capern visited Stoneleigh Abbey on a 'delightful April day, when the sun shone upon it and its surroundings with its blandest beams', walking there across fields and through woods from Kenilworth station. As there is no longer a railway station at Kenilworth and their route nowadays would entail walking along suburban roads, this walk approaches the grand house at Stoneleigh from the small nearby village of Ashow. Note that the walk is only possible when the grounds and house are open to the public, which is from the beginning of April to the end of October on Tuesday, Wednesday, Thursday, Sunday and Bank Holidays. Details of opening times can be checked either by phoning 01926 858535 or visiting www.stoneleighabbey.org.

The Walk

The lane through the quiet and secluded village of Ashow is a cul de sac; the only way out is the way you came in, apart from a path that leads past the church to a footbridge across the River Avon. The medieval church, one of the oldest in Warwickshire, occupies a fine position overlooking the river. It still retains much of its original Norman work but has been rebuilt and restored several times over the centuries.

Ashow's medieval church is situated beside the River Avon

1. It is worthwhile either before the start or at the end of the walk to make the brief detour along the public footpath that leads off to the right at the end of the lane to visit the old church and enjoy the view from the footbridge over the Avon.

    Begin the walk by going back along the lane through the village to the B4115, cross over and take the tree-lined, tarmac track opposite. The track later narrows to a sunken path and on approaching the A46, widens into a track again, bends right and then turns left to cross a footbridge over the dual carriageway. Continue along another tree-lined track to a road on the edge of Kenilworth.

2. Turn right and after ¼ mile (0.4 km) – just after passing the entrance to Kenilworth Wardens Sports Club – look out for a public footpath sign on the right and take a narrow path into trees. The path bends left, keeping by the boundary fence of the sports club, and continues through woodland to a T-junction. Turn right, recross the busy A46 and continue through woodland to emerge, via a stile, onto the B4115 again opposite the entrance to Stoneleigh Abbey.

3. Walk along the tree-lined drive, crossing a bridge over the Avon, and continue to the entrance to the house and grounds.

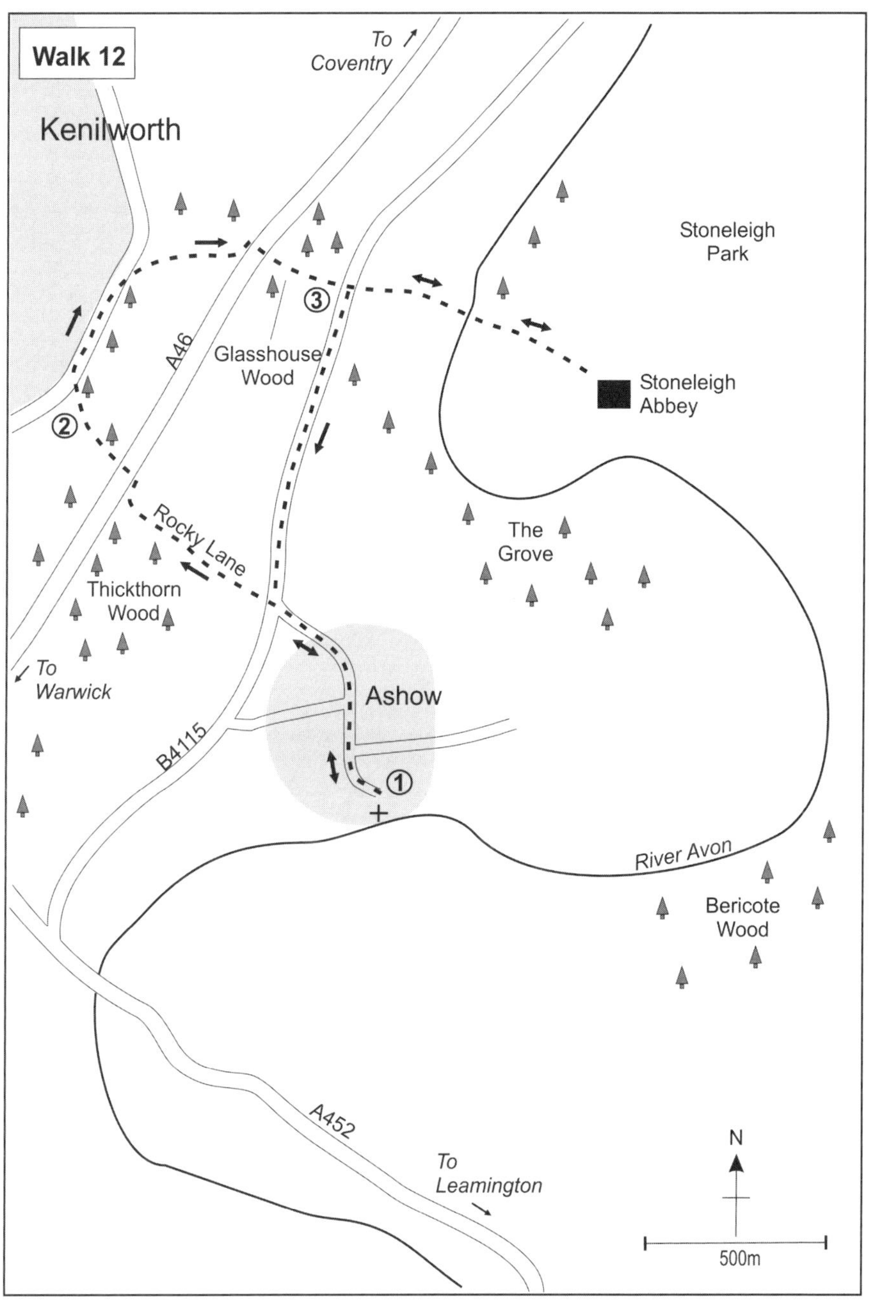

Walk 12
Kenilworth
To Coventry
Stoneleigh Park
A46
Glasshouse Wood
3
Stoneleigh Abbey
2
Rocky Lane
The Grove
Thickthorn Wood
To Warwick
B4115
Ashow
1
River Avon
Bericote Wood
A452
To Leamington
N
500m

As the name suggests, Stoneleigh Abbey was built on the site of a medieval abbey and the former monastic gatehouse is where you enter.

West Wing of Stoneleigh Abbey

After the dissolution of the monasteries, it came into the possession of the Leigh family in 1561 and remained in their ownership until 1996. Much of the Tudor house that was built on the site survives and is now divided into private apartments. In the early 18th century a new and imposing West Wing was built on the front of it and this is the part of the house that is open to the public. Burritt describes the West Wing as a

The River Avon winds through Stoneleigh Park

Former monastic gatehouse at Stoneleigh Abbey

'stately, large, and elegant building, of modern structure and style, such as a block of the same length taken from the Rue Rivoli in Paris, or from the terraces of the West End of London would look if transported and planted in a rural landscape'.

The house occupies a beautiful spot by the River Avon and Burritt concentrated his remarks on the exterior and setting of the house and the adjoining parkland. This is because 'As Lord Leigh was at home, we did not ask permission to see the interior of the house; which, from published accounts, must be fitted up with great taste, with all the luxuries and adornments which wealth can command'

Retrace your steps back along the drive to the B4115, (3) turn left – there are verges both side of the road – and after ½ mile (800m), take the first lane on the left, signposted to Ashow. Here you pick up the outward route and retrace your steps to the start.

13. Leamington to Warwick

'Really the only baronial castle that has survived destruction or decay'

Distance	3 ½ miles (5.6 km)
Approximate time	2 hours
Start	Leamington, Pump Rooms at the bottom of the Parade, grid ref SP318655
Finish	Warwick, Market Place, grid ref SP281650
Parking	Warwick
Terrain	Clear and easy paths and tracks mainly by rivers, with one short stretch of canal towpath
Refreshments	Pubs, cafes and restaurants at Leamington; pubs, cafes and restaurants at Warwick
Public Transport	Buses from Stratford-upon-Avon, Coventry and most surrounding towns; trains from Birmingham
Map	OS Explorer 221 (Coventry & Warwick)

A combination of three waterways – the River Leam, Grand Union Canal and River Avon – creates an attractive and peaceful green corridor that links the adjacent and contrasting towns of Leamington and Warwick. Elihu Burritt visited both towns during the course of his journeys through the 'green borderland' and was predictably enthusiastic about both of them, especially the castle, church and other historic buildings of Warwick. This is the only linear walk in the book but all you have to do is to catch a bus from Warwick bus station just off the Market Place – there is a frequent service between the towns – get off at the Parade in Leamington and walk down to the Pump Rooms, the starting point of the walk.

The Walk

Elihu Burritt described Leamington – or to give the town its full title, Royal Leamington Spa – as a 'kind of Saratoga', a similar spa town in New York State, and declared that it was 'a resort for invalids of mild indisposition'. At the time of his visit, it was still a fairly recent town, little more than a village until the discovery of mineral springs in the 1780s. After that it grew rapidly and still retains many elegant Regency and Victorian terraces and crescents and the many attractive parks and gardens that date from its heyday as a spa. The Pump Rooms are one of its most prominent buildings. They were first opened in 1814 with 20 baths but were extended several times in the Victorian era.

1. Start by facing the Pump Rooms and take the path to the right of them to enter the Pump Rooms Gardens. At the end of the building, bear right onto a path that keeps along the edge of the gardens beside the River Leam on the left and turn left to cross a footbridge over the river. Turn right up steps and continue along a broad, tree-lined path through Victoria Park on the

The 19th century Pump Rooms at Leamington

other bank of the Leam. Pass under a road bridge, keep ahead, and immediately after passing under a second bridge (a railway bridge), cross a road to a Riverside Walk sign opposite. Walk along an enclosed path, continue across a field, bearing slightly left away from the river, and the path becomes enclosed again and keeps above a railway line on the left to emerge onto the towpath of the Grand Union Canal.

   The Grand Union Canal was formed as a result of amalgamations between several smaller canal companies. It runs for 137 miles (220 km) between Little Venice in London and Gas Street Basin in Birmingham.

2. Turn right and at a footpath sign 'Link to Riverside Walk' – just after crossing an aqueduct over the River Avon – turn right and descend a

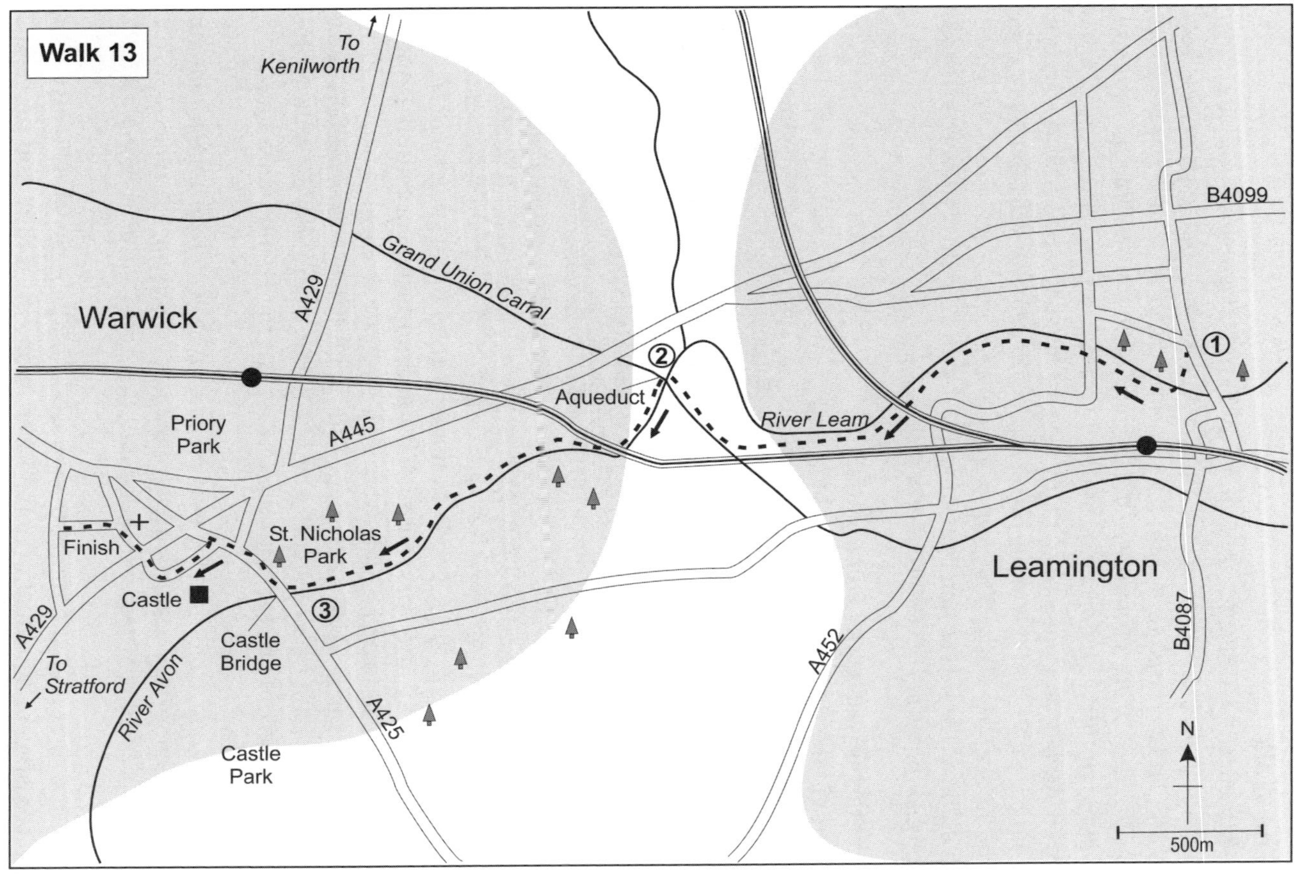

Walk 13
To Kenilworth
Grand Union Canal
B4099
Warwick
A429
Priory Park
A445
Aqueduct
2
River Leam
1
Finish
St. Nicholas Park
Castle
3
Castle Bridge
A429
To Stratford
River Avon
Castle Park
A425
Leamington
A452
B4087
N
500m

flight of steps. Turn right again at the bottom along a wooded path, pass under the aqueduct and continue beside the Avon. After emerging from the trees, walk across a grassy area, cross a track to the right of a bridge and continue beside the river along the edge of St Nicholas Park. Soon the towers and walls of Warwick Castle can be seen across the meadows on the right. Keep by the river to Castle Bridge, ascend steps beside it up to a road and turn left to see the classic view of the castle.

The view of Warwick Castle from the bridge, its walls and towers rising above the River Avon, can justifiably claim to be one of the finest in the country. Burritt described it as the only baronial castle to have survived largely intact but there are a few others - notably Alnwick and Arundel - that have made the transition from castle to stately home. The castle was started soon after the Norman Conquest but the present building

Warwick Castle from the River Avon

dates mainly from the 14th century. During the 17th, 18th and 19th centuries it was extensively rebuilt and modernised and much of the interior was reconstructed to transform it from a draughty medieval fortress into a comfortable palatial residence. The state rooms contain many impressive paintings and items of furniture and there is a particularly extensive collection of arms and armour. In addition there are attractive gardens to explore.

3. After admiring the view, turn right along the road, passing the end of picturesque Mill Street, and just before reaching the road junction by the East Gate, turn left along Castle Lane. At a T-junction, turn right along pedestrianised Castle Street, cross over the main road and keep ahead up Church Street to St Mary's Church. Turn left and the street leads into the Market Place, the end of the walk.

In the 1860s Burritt wrote 'Warwick is not all castle. Far from it. It is a goodly, venerable town with a public character and history distinct from

West Gate and Lord Leycester hospital at Warwick

St Mary's Chuch, Warwick

the castle'. This is still true today and Burritt particularly singled out St Mary's Church and the Lord Leycester Hospital.

The large medieval church of St Mary, dominated by its imposing tower, was all but destroyed in a disastrous fire that swept through the town in 1694 and had to be rebuilt during the reign of Queen Anne. Fortunately the 15th century Beauchamp Chapel survived the fire. In it are the tombs of several Earls of Warwick but particularly outstanding is the tomb of Robert Dudley, Earl of Leicester, the favourite of Elizabeth I and owner of the nearby castle at Kenilworth.

The picturesque, timber-framed Lord Leycester Hospital, located near the end of the walk, is a group of almshouses built in the late 14th century next to the West Gate into the town. Above it is a 12th century chapel. It was originally built as a guildhall but became a retirement home for ex-serviceman and their wives during the reign of Elizabeth I and still serves that purpose today.

14. Stratford-upon-Avon and Shottery

'Is there another town in Christendom to equal it for the centripetal attraction of one human memory?'

Distance	4 ½ miles (7.2 km)
Approximate time	2 hours
Start	Stratford-upon-Avon, by Shakespeare's statue, grid ref SP205549
Parking	Stratford-upon-Avon
Terrain	Flat walking mostly along tarmac and riverside paths
Refreshments	Pubs, cafes and restaurants at Stratford-upon-Avon
Public Transport	Buses from Birmingham, Coventry, Leamington, Warwick and most local towns and villages; trains from Birmingham
Map	OS Explorer 205 (Stratford-upon-Avon & Evesham)

On the first part of this walk you may well be following in the footsteps of both Shakespeare and Elihu Burritt. It takes you across what were formerly the 'daisied fields', as Burritt describes them, between Stratford and the childhood home of Anne Hathaway, Shakespeare's wife, in the hamlet of Shottery. Now these fields are no more as the 20th century suburban spread of Stratford has turned most of them into manicured recreation grounds surrounded by modern housing but nevertheless it is still a pleasant, quiet and green walk. After a visit to Anne Hathaway's Cottage at Shottery, the return to Stratford is along the banks of the River Avon, passing the church in which Shakespeare is buried and the Royal Shakespeare Theatre.

The Walk

1. With your back to the road, turn right beside the canal, go up steps onto the road and turn left to cross the canal bridge. Keep ahead up Bridge Street and at a road junction in front of Barclays Bank, take the road to the right of the bank building (Henley Street) which brings you to Shakespeare's birthplace.

Shakespeare's Birthplace in Henley Street, Stratford

William Shakespeare was born in this substantial 16th century town house in 1564, the son of a wool merchant and glove maker. The birthplace is just one of a number of Shakespearean properties in Stratford that attract literary pilgrims from all over the world. These include: the remains and gardens of New Place, where Shakespeare lived during the latter part of his life after finding fame and fortune in London; Hall's Croft, where his daughter Susanna and her husband lived; the Grammar School that he attended and Holy Trinity Church where he is buried. Just outside the town is Anne Hathaway's Cottage, the childhood home of his wife at Shottery; and Mary Arden's House at Wilmcote, where his mother was brought up and lived until her marriage to Shakespeare's father.

The world wide popularity of Shakespeare had put Stratford firmly on the tourist map by the 1860s when Burritt visited the town. He writes: 'the memory of Shakespeare covers with its disk the whole life and being and history, ancient and modern, of Stratford-upon-Avon. There is nothing seen or felt before or behind it but William Shakespeare. In no quarter of the globe, since he was laid to his last sleep by the sunny side of the peaceful river, has the name of the little town been mentioned without suggesting and meaning him'. It is true that in Stratford you cannot

Just before reaching the house, the route continues to the left along Meer Street to a road junction. Cross over to the clock tower and continue past it down Rother Street into Evesham Place. Bear right onto a path across a rectangular area of grass and trees (The Firs Gardens), cross the road that skirts the other side of the green and at the apex of the triangle turn right – there is a footpath sign to Anne Hathaway's Cottage – along an enclosed tarmac track.

2. Continue in a straight line along enclosed tarmac paths, crossing a succession of suburban roads, and after crossing a footbridge over a brook, the route continues across the middle of a playing field. At a fork, take the right hand path which curves right to the far end of the field. Walk along an enclosed path and at the next fork, continue along the left hand path, signposted to Anne Hathaway's Cottage via Shottery. The path emerges onto a road. Turn right and the road immediately bends left into Shottery. At a junction the route continues to the left along Hathaway Lane but in order to make the short detour to Anne Hathaway's Cottage, keep ahead and follow the road to the right by the Bell Inn. At a crossroads either turn left and follow the road to the cottage, or for a more attractive alternative, cross the road, turn left into a path through gardens which bends right beside Shottery Brook, turn left to cross a footbridge over the brook and the cottage is immediately ahead.

Anne Hathaway's Cottage at Shottery

Cottage is really a false description for this reasonably spacious and picturesque Tudor

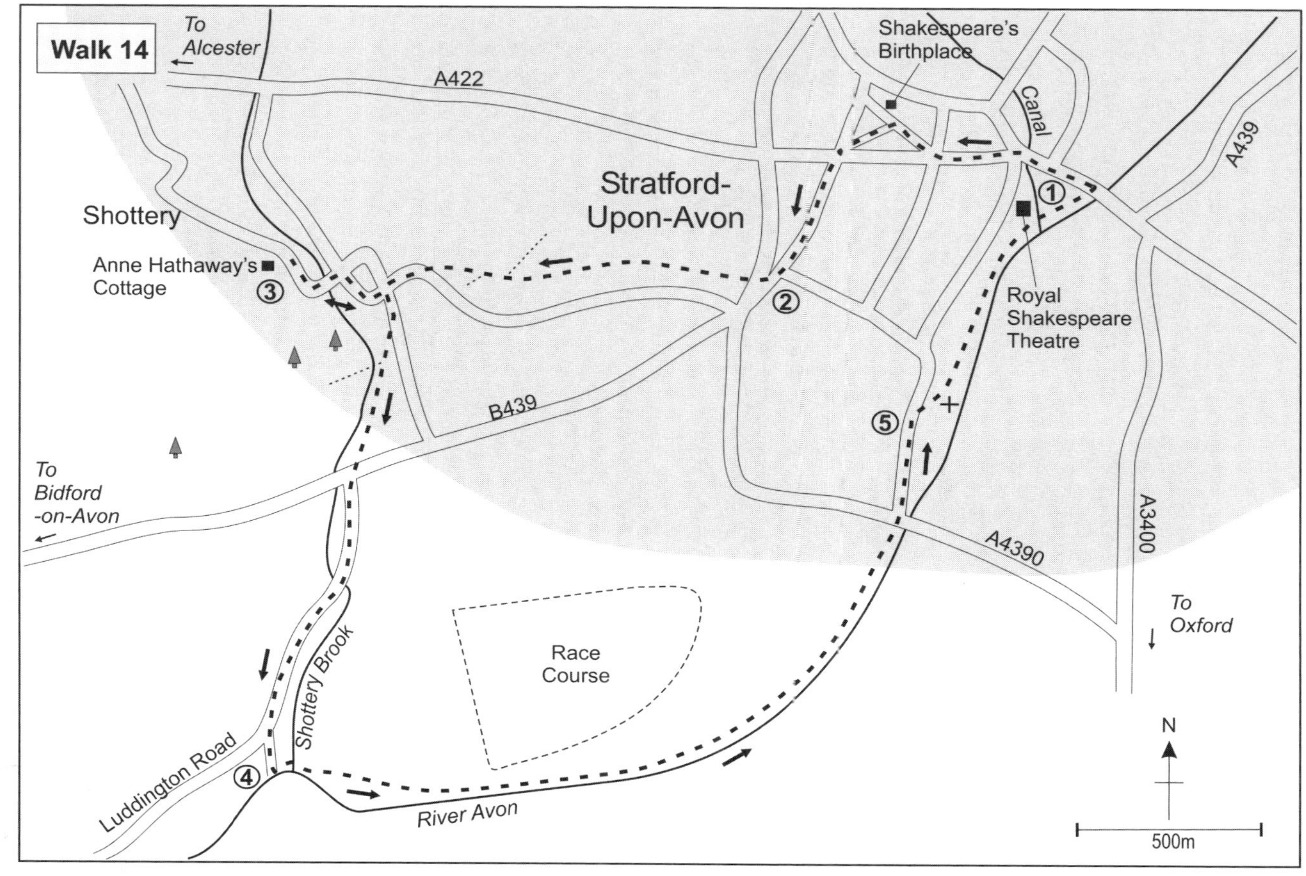

Walk 14
To Alcester
Shakespeare's Birthplace
A422
Canal
A439
Stratford-Upon-Avon
Shottery
Anne Hathaway's Cottage
③
①
②
Royal Shakespeare Theatre
⑤
B439
To Bidford -on-Avon
A4390
A3400
To Oxford
Shottery Brook
Luddington Road
④
River Avon
Race Course
N
500m

farmhouse which was the childhood home of Shakespeare's wife, Anne Hathaway. She was eight years his senior and they were married in 1582 when William was 18 and Anne was 26. Anne died in 1623, seven years after her husband.

3. Retrace your steps to Hathaway Lane and turn along it. At a public footpath sign, turn right along an enclosed track to Brookfield Nursery and where the track curves slightly right just before the nursery, turn left along a tarmac track to a road. Continue along the road (Hogarth Road) and where it ends, keep ahead along a tree-lined path beside Shottery Brook to a main road. Cross over and continue along the road opposite (Luddington Road), passing the entrance to Stratford Racecourse. Where the road bends right, turn left into Stannells Close and where it ends, turn left onto a path beside a house. The path bends first to the right and then to the left to reach the bank of the River Avon.

4. Keep along an enclosed path beside the river and after crossing a footbridge over a brook, continue along the edge of a riverside meadow. Go through a kissing gate at the far end of the meadow – the racecourse is over to the left – pass under the arches of a disused railway bridge and continue by the Avon to a road bridge. On this stretch of the walk the spire of Holy Trinity Church at Stratford comes into view. After passing under the bridge, the path rises gently to a road and you keep along it to enter the churchyard of Holy Trinity.

    In this impressive medieval church, visited by thousands of people every year, Shakespeare was baptised in 1564 and buried in 1616. His grave can be seen in the chancel and Anne Hathaway is buried alongside him.

Shakespeare's statue by the river at Stratford

Royal Shakespeare Theatre and Holy Trinity Church at Stratford

5. Walk past the church to the river and turn left to keep beside it. Go through a gate to exit the churchyard and continue along a path, between the river and road, passing in front of the Royal Shakespeare Theatre.

The Royal Shakespeare Theatre first opened in 1879 as the Shakespeare Memorial Theatre but most of this building was destroyed by a fire in 1926. Its replacement, which was built in 1932, has recently undergone a major reconstruction, including the building of a tower. It reopened in 2010.

Continue across the Bancroft Gardens towards the Tramway Bridge and just before reaching it, cross a bridge over the canal. The starting point by Shakespeare's statue is just to the left.

15. Lickey Hills

'There are no hills more grateful and delightful for airing one's body and soul than the Lickey cluster'

Distance	4 ½ miles (7.2 km)
Approximate time	2 ½ hours
Start	Lickey Hills Country Park Visitor Centre, signposted from the B4096 between Rednal and Bromsgrove, grid ref SO998755
Parking	Lickey Hills Country Park
Terrain	Open hillside and woodland, two ascents and descents
Refreshments	Café at Visitor Centre, café at golf club car park
Public Transport	None
Map	OS Explorers 219 (Wolverhampton & Dudley) and 220 (Birmingham)

It is obvious from the above quotation that Elihu Burritt was very fond of the Lickeys, a feeling shared by thousands of Brummies about the nearest range of hills to the city. In his book he reminisces about a walk that he did to there on his first visit to England in 1846 when he started from Edgbaston and stayed at the Rose and Crown, describing it as 'a snug, quiet little hotel......just the English wayside inn I had read and dreamed of from youth'. In 1863-64 he returned to complete the walk that

The Rose and Crown at the foot of the Lickeys, Elihu Burritt's 'little cosy old inn'

he had embarked upon 17 years before and was equally enthralled by the hills, although even the most patriotic Brummie might feel that he was going a little over the top when he wrote that they are 'perfectly Scotch in cut and clothing' and that these 'remarkable hills look as if transplanted here from the Highlands'. The range comprises four main hills – Cofton, Bilberry, Rednal and Beacon – and this walk embraces three of them. It takes the form of a figure of eight based on the visitor centre. On the first circuit you descend the wooded Cofton Hill and head across to Cofton Hackett Church before climbing back to the start. The second half takes you across Bilberry Hill, descends to the Rose and Crown and then ascends to the toposcope on Beacon Hill, the highest point on the Lickeys and a superb viewpoint.

The Walk

For many generations of Brummies, the Lickey Hills were the foremost local weekend and Bank Holiday destination, especially in the days – before 1952 – when one of the highlights of the trip was a ride along Bristol Road on the number 70 tram from the city centre to the Rednal terminus. In the Middle Ages the area belonged to the manor of Bromsgrove but in the 16th century it was granted by the Crown to the Earls of Plymouth. It was during the Victorian era that the hills first became a popular recreation area, as Burritt indicates, and in 1888 Rednal Hill was given to the city of Birmingham. Later gifts of land by the philanthropic Cadbury family and purchases from the Earl of Plymouth extended the area owned by the city to the present 525 acres. The hills are now a country park and comprise a mixture of woodland, grassland and heathland.

1. From the front of the visitor centre, turn right up to the car park and turn right again along a broad track. At a sign to Cofton Hill and a red-waymarked post beside gates, bear right along a track which immediately plunges into woodland. The track later descends through the lovely Cofton Woods, curving left and continuing down to a junction of paths at the bottom. Turn right parallel to a road and at a T-junction, turn left and pass beside a gate onto the road. Cross over, turn right and almost immediately turn left along Cofton Church Lane and follow it for just over ½ mile (0.8 km) to Cofton Hackett Church.

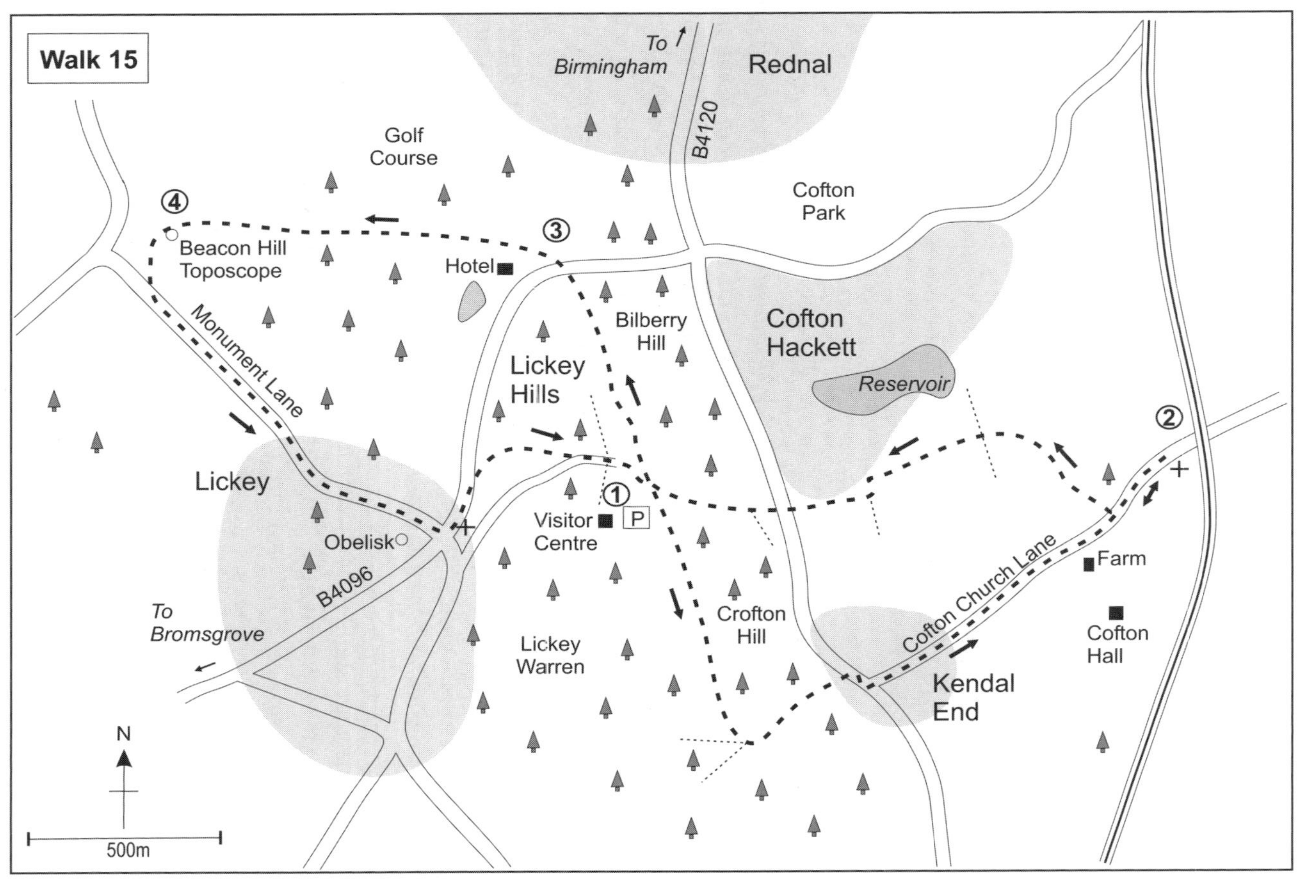

To Birmingham
Rednal
B4120
Golf Course
Cofton Park
Cofton Hackett
Reservoir
Beacon Hill Toposcope
Hotel
Bilberry Hill
Lickey Hills
Monument Lane
Lickey
Obelisk
B4096
To Bromsgrove
Visitor Centre
P
Lickey Warren
Crofton Hill
Cofton Church Lane
Farm
Cofton Hall
Kendal End
N
500m

The small church at Cofton Hackett

This small church, originally a chapel, has the feel of a remote country church rather than one on the edge of Britain's second city. It was mostly rebuilt in 1861 but retains some of its earlier medieval stonework.

2. Retrace your steps for 100 yards (91m) and at a public footpath sign, turn right onto a path that heads gently uphill by the right edge of a field. The path bends left and continues to a kissing gate. Go through, and another one directly opposite, continue along the right edge of two fields and go through a gate on the far side of the second field. Walk along an enclosed path to a road, cross over to a public footpath sign opposite and take an uphill path through woodland. At the top of a flight of steps, turn right onto a track which continues up the thickly wooded slopes of Cofton Hill, curving left to reach the car park by the visitor centre. (1)

For the second part of this figure of eight walk, turn right onto the broad track used at the start of the walk and at the end of the parking area, turn right along a gently ascending path. Turn left at a waymarked post and walk along a ridge top path which descends to join a clear track. Continue along it over Bilberry Hill, enjoying the fine views, head downhill through trees and finally descend a long flight of steps to a road.

3. Cross over, turn left and make your way across the gardens adjoining the Rose and Crown Hotel (Burritt's 'snug, quiet English wayside inn') to the car park at the back. Here the ascent of Beacon Hill begins by picking up a tarmac path, signposted to Monument Lane and Toposcope. Pass beside a barrier, head uphill and at the top end of the field, head through a belt of trees and go up steps to a track. Turn right along it, follow the wide main track around a left bend at a junction and at the next junction, turn right, in the direction of a footpath sign to Toposcope. At a fork take the right hand path, bending right where another path joins from the left, and take the right hand path again at the next fork. At the next fork, continue uphill through woodland along the left hand path, finally emerging from the trees and heading across open grassland to the toposcope on the summit of Beacon Hill.

Birmingham owes much to the generosity of the Cadbury family

At 975 feet (298 m), Beacon Hill is the highest point on the Lickey Hills and provides magnificent views both across the city and over a large slice of rural Worcestershire. A comprehensive direction indicator reveals the many landmarks that can be seen from here in clear conditions. This battlemented structure was a gift from the Cadbury family.

4. From the toposcope, turn left across the grass, pass through a car park to a road and turn left. After nearly ¾ mile (1.2 km) you reach a crossroads and opposite is Lickey church.

    In the churchyard of this Victorian church is the grave of Herbert Austin, founder of the Austin Motor Company and one of the great pioneers of the British car industry. He established his factory down the road from here at Longbridge, formerly a major landmark on the journey from Birmingham city centre out to the Lickeys.

    Turn left and turn right along the track, signposted to Visitor Centre, to return to the start.

16. Clent Hills: Four Stones and Wychbury Hill

'This lofty watch-tower on the Green Borderland'

Distance	4 ½ miles (7.2 km)
Approximate time	2 ½ hours
Start	Clent Hills, Nimmings Wood car park, signposted from the A456 between Halesowen and Hagley, grid ref SO 939807
Parking	Nimmings Wood
Terrain	Two ascents and descents – steady rather than steep and strenuous – and clear, well-signed paths across fields and through woods
Refreshments	Kiosk at Nimmings Wood
Public Transport	None to start, but you could start the walk at Hagley which is served by buses from Birmingham, Halesowen and Kidderminmster
Map	OS Explorer 219 (Wolverhampton & Dudley)

It is not hard to see why Elihu Burritt referred to the Clent Hills as a 'lofty watch-tower on the Green Borderland'. Right from the start even the view from the car park is superb and from the higher points the views become even more impressive and extensive. Two of the finest viewpoints are from the Four Stones on the summit of Clent Hill and from near the monument on Wychbury Hill. In between there is much attractive woodland walking and glimpses of a great house.

View over the Black Country from the start of the walk

The Walk

Writing in 1868, Elihu Burritt comments that the Clent Hills are a 'favourite resort and breathing ground of miners and forgers and the other sooty workers of the Black Country' where they can 'quaff the luxury of the happiest and healthiest air that breathes, and disport themselves to their hearts content in all the wild freedom of the place.' There may not be so many miners, forgers and other sooty workers nowadays but the people of the Black Country and surrounding area still flock to enjoy these hills on fine weekends and the decline of heavy industry means that the views are considerably clearer than when Burritt came here. This grand walking and cycling area is now under the protection of the National Trust.

1. Exit the car park, turn right and almost immediately turn right again through a waymarked kissing gate. Climb steps through woodland,

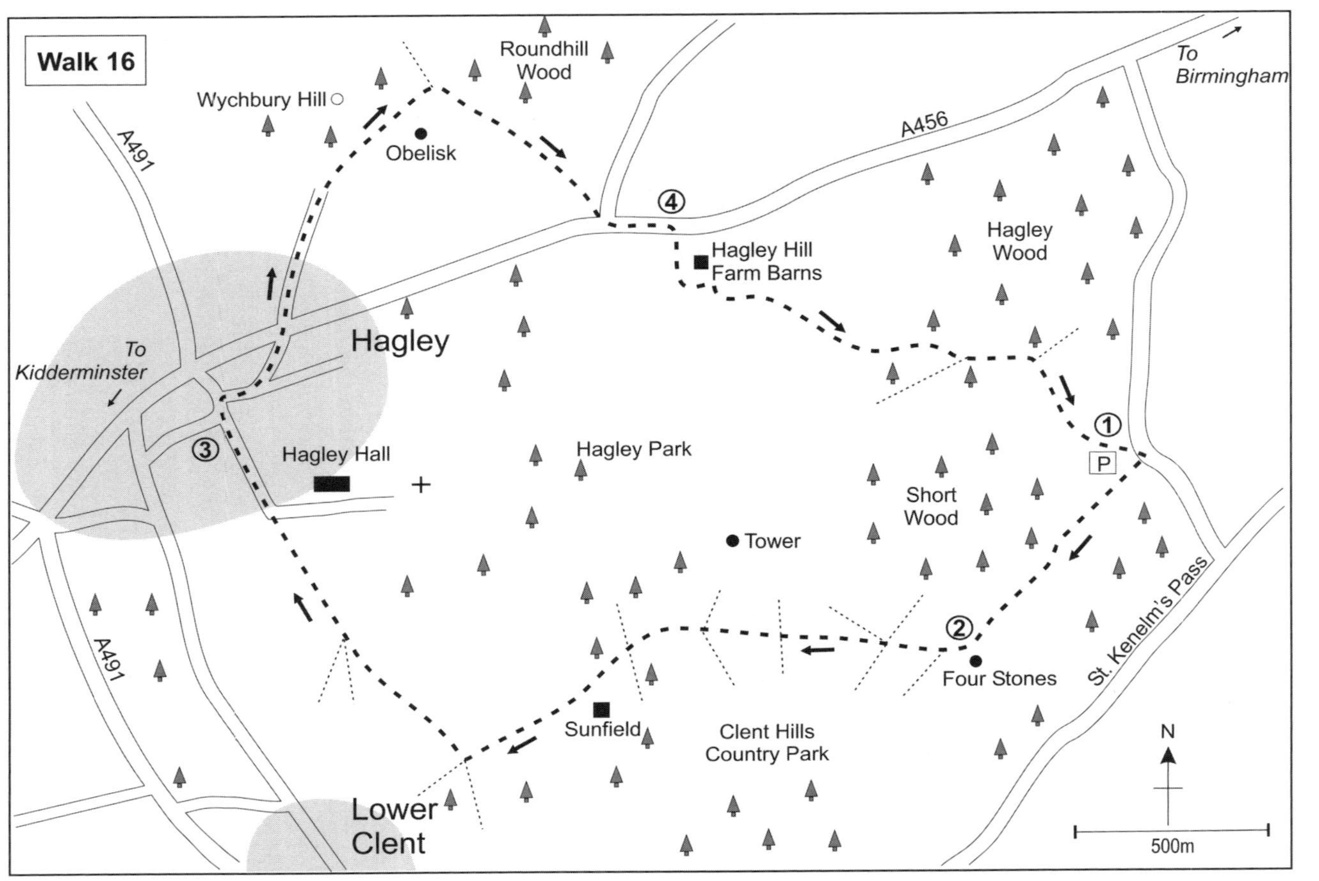

Walk 16
Roundhill Wood
Wychbury Hill
To Birmingham
A456
Obelisk
4
Hagley Wood
A491
Hagley Hill Farm Barns
To Kidderminster
Hagley
1
P
3
Hagley Hall
Hagley Park
Short Wood
Tower
St. Kenelm's Pass
2
Four Stones
A491
Sunfield
Clent Hills Country Park
Lower Clent
N
500m

continue uphill and the path levels off and continues to a kissing gate. Go through and keep ahead through more open country along a broad, undulating track to the Four Stones.

Although they look like a mini Stonehenge, the Four Stones are a folly, placed here in the 18th century by the 1st Lord Lyttleton, builder of nearby Hagley Hall, and his poet friend, William Shenstone, creator of the landscaped garden at The Leasowes near Halesowen. Their motive was to improve the view of the hills and they are one of a number of follies scattered throughout Hagley Park. At a height of 997 feet (315m), the views from here are magnificent, extending in a wide arc over the Black Country and across rural Worcestershire to the Clee, Abberley and Malvern hills.

2. Bear right at the stones, take the right hand track at a fork and head gently downhill. Cross a track, passing a toposcope, and continue

The Four Stones, a folly on top of the Clent Hills

downhill, following North Worcestershire Path waymarks. The track later narrows to a path and continues downhill through woodland, later becoming steeper, into a dip. Turn right and continue along the right inside edge of the trees to a T-junction. Turn left along an enclosed path and on reaching a tarmac drive, turn right and continue along a hedge-lined track. At a junction of paths, turn right along another tree- and hedge-lined path, pass beside a barrier and keep ahead. Glimpses of Hagley Hall can be seen through the trees on the right. Eventually you pass beside another barrier and keep ahead to emerge onto a road on the edge of Hagley.

The great Palladian mansion of Hagley Hall was built in the 18th century by Lord Lyttleton and has a fine collection of paintings and furniture. Although the interior was badly damaged by fire in 1925, it has been subsequently restored to its former glory. As well as the mock prehistoric stones already seen, the follies in the adjoining park include

Looking down on Hagley Hall from Wychbury Hill

3. Continue along the road, follow it around a right bend (School Lane)
    and the road curves left to the main road (A456). Cross carefully, turn
    right and almost immediately turn left and head gently uphill along
    Monument Lane. The lane later becomes an enclosed track which
    continues up to a kissing gate. Go through, keep ahead to a footpath
    post where you go through a gate and continue gently uphill below
    woodland on the right to a stile. Climb it and keep ahead along the
    right edge of the trees that crown Wychbury Hill, 734 feet (224m) high,
    site of an Iron Age fort and another fine viewpoint. The obelisk on the
    right is another of the Hagley Park follies. In the field corner, climb the
    stile in front and turn right by a wire fence on the right, heading gently
    downhill. Turn right over another stile in that fence, turn left and
    continue, now with the fence and hedge on the left, to a kissing gate.
    Go through and go up steps to emerge again onto the A456. Turn left,
    cross a side road (Wassell Grove) and when you see a tarmac path on
    the right pointing the way across the busy dual carriageway, cross
    carefully and turn left on the other side.

4. At a hedge gap turn right over a stile, take the path ahead across a
    field, turn right through a kissing gate in the corner and turn left onto
    an enclosed track. Where the track bends right, keep ahead through a
    gap, by a yellow-waymarked post, later curving left to enter Hagley
    Wood. Immediately follow a path to the right, heading up to climb a
    stile on the edge of the trees. Turn left across a field towards the right
    corner of woodland, climb a stile, keep ahead over another one and
    walk gently uphill across a field to a kissing gate. Go through, head up
    through trees to go through another one and continue uphill across
    the next field to go through one more kissing gate. Keep ahead along
    a path that leads up through trees back to the start.

17. Clent Hills: St Kenelm's Church and Walton Hill

'These bald and breezy heights'

Distance	3 ½ miles (5.6 km)
Approximate time	2 hours
Start	Clent Hills, Nimmings Wood car park, signposted from the A456 between Halesowen and Hagley, grid ref SO 939807
Parking	Nimmings Wood
Terrain	Two steady ascents and descents, field paths and woodland tracks, some of which may be muddy
Refreshments	Kiosk at Nimmings Wood
Public Transport	None
Map	OS Explorer 219 (Wolverhampton & Dudley)

The Clent Hills are such superb walking country within easy reach of Birmingham and the Black Country that they merit two walks. This second route takes you to the small and secluded church of St Kenelm before heading up through woodland to the summit of Walton Hill, at 1035 feet (315m), the highest point on the Clent range and inevitably a magnificent viewpoint. A wooded descent brings you to Clent Church and a final climb – still through woodland – leads up to the other grand viewpoint of the Four Stones. From here it is just a short distance back to the start.

The Walk

1. Exit the car park, climb a stile on the opposite side of the lane and turn right along the right field edge. Turn left in the corner, head downhill

and near the bottom right hand corner of the field, look out for where you turn right over a waymarked stile. Keep ahead to climb another stile, continue across the next field, go through a hedge gap and continue across to a kissing gate. Go through, cross a small field, go through a belt of trees into the churchyard of St Kenelm's Church and turn left to the church.

St Kenelm's Church

This small sandstone church is built on the site of the alleged martyrdom of St Kenelm, a 9th century boy prince of Mercia. It mainly dates from the 15th century but was heavily restored in the 19th century. A spring in a hollow just below the church is supposed to mark the exact spot where the foul murder took place. According to legend, the body was later miraculously discovered and taken to the abbey of Winchcombe in the Cotswolds for burial.

2. Pass to the right of the church, go through a gate and immediately turn right through another one and walk along a narrow path to a road. Turn left and at a T-junction, turn right uphill, in the Romsley and Hunnington direction. Where the road curves left, keep ahead to a public footpath sign, climb a stile and head gently uphill across a field towards woodland. Climb steps on the far side, go through a gate and keep ahead to a lane. Turn left, take the right hand lane at a fork and just ahead, turn right through a gate. Continue along a path that climbs steadily through woodland, eventually emerging from the trees into open country on the summit of Walton Hill, and head across to the trig point.

The summit of Walton Hill, 1035 feet (315m), is the highest point on the Clent Hills. The magnificent views from here take in the Wrekin and the

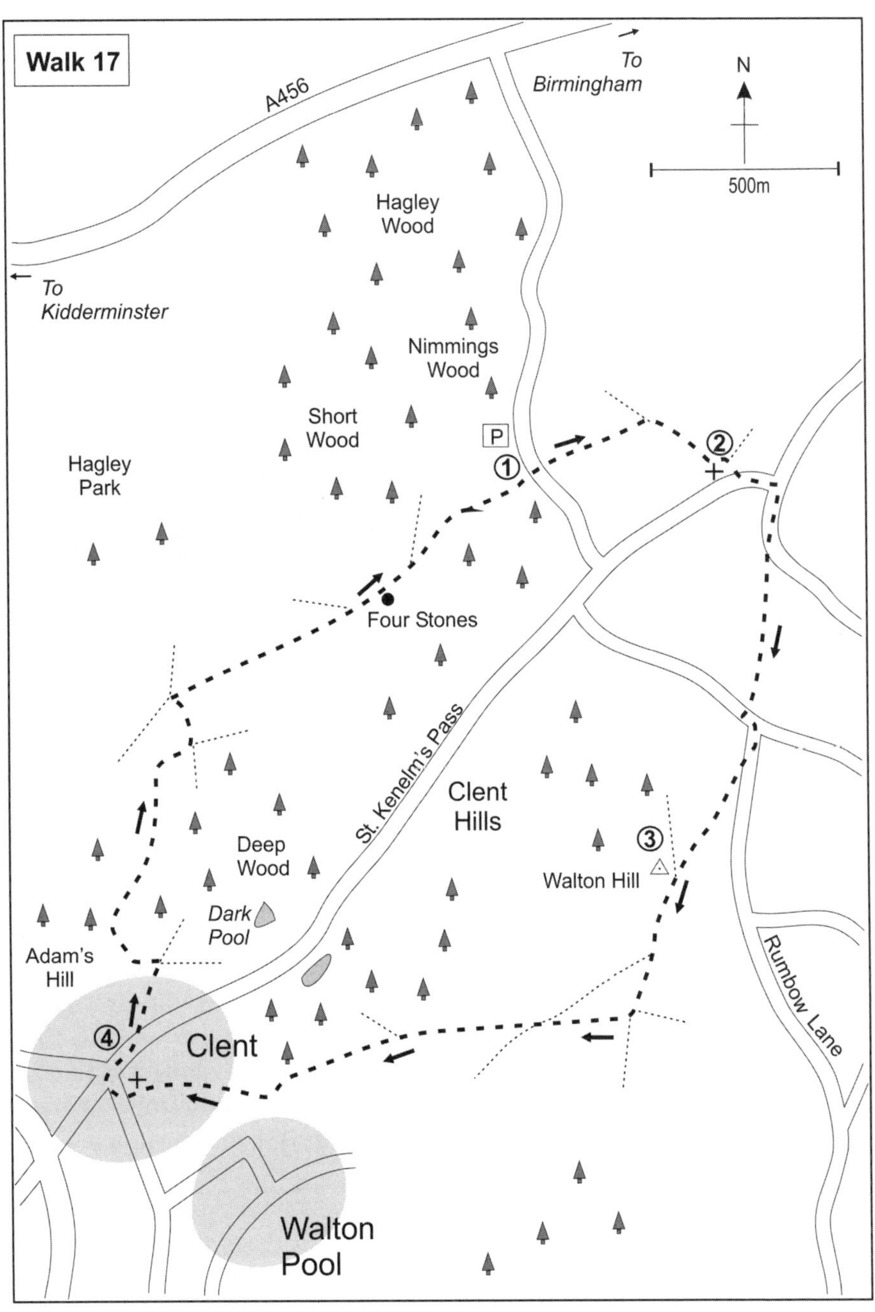

Walk 17
A456
To Birmingham
N
500m
To Kidderminster
Hagley Wood
Nimmings Wood
Short Wood
P
①
②
Hagley Park
Four Stones
St. Kenelm's Pass
Clent Hills
③
Walton Hill
Deep Wood
Dark Pool
Adam's Hill
④
Clent
Rumbow Lane
Walton Pool

Summit of Walton Hill, highest point on the Clent Hills

Cotswold, Malvern, Clee and Abberley hills and, on clear days, even extend to the Black Mountains in south Wales.

3. Turn left and ahead are two paths. The route continues along the right hand one which keeps along the right edge of the open grassy area, later descending steadily through woodland. At a fork take the right hand path – the footpath not the bridleway – and continue down to a kissing gate on the edge of the trees. Go through, keep ahead along a grassy ridge, descending to go through another kissing gate and continue more steeply down to a gate. Go through, turn left along a narrow path beside the wall of Clent churchyard to a lane and keep ahead to a crossroads in front of the church.

Like St Kenelm's, the medieval church at Clent is built of sandstone. The tower was added in the 15th century and the church was thoroughly restored and partially rebuilt in the Victorian era.

4. Turn right along Vine Lane and at a public bridleway sign, turn left along a track and continue past the end of a cottage, heading uphill. At a fork take the left hand upper path and climb steeply through woodland to a crossways. Turn left and continue uphill, curving right and then descending slightly to a junction of paths and tracks.

Clent Church

Turn right uphill again, emerging into open country, and at a junction where the path ahead starts to descend, turn left onto a gently ascending path. On reaching a broad track, turn right along it to the Four Stones.

Looking towards the Malverns from Walton Hill

For information on the Four Stones, refer to Walk 16

Keep to the left of the stones, continue along the broad, undulating track to where it ends and go through a kissing gate into woodland. Keep ahead, later descending steps, and go through a kissing gate onto a road. The car park is just to the left.

18. The Leasowes

'Winding walks over stream and pool and under overarching trees'

Distance	2 ½ miles (4 km)
Approximate time	1 ½ hours
Start	Leasowes Park, off the A458 just to the east of Halesowen town centre, grid ref SO 976841
Parking	Leasowes Park
Terrain	Apart from two short stretches beside a canal, mostly on clear paths through woodland and a landscaped garden
Refreshments	None
Public Transport	Buses from Birmingham, Halesowen and Kidderminster
Map	OS Explorer 219 (Wolverhampton & Dudley)

The Leasowes, situated on the fringes of Birmingham and the Black Country, sandwiched between two busy main roads and scarcely a stone's throw from the M5 motorway, is an unlikely setting for a nationally renowned 18th century landscaped garden. The heyday of the garden was during the late 18th and early 19th centuries and it was already past its best when Elihu Burritt, together with his friend and companion Edward Capern, visited it towards the end of a November ramble from Old Hill to Halesowen and then back home to Harborne. Burritt was particularly interested in William Shenstone, the creator of the garden, having just visited his grave in Halesowen churchyard. By the time he arrived at The Leasowes around sunset there was little time for an exploration, although he does comment on the view from there of the Clent Hills 'tinged with the rich purple mist in which the setting sun was sinking in the west.' The walk begins with a stroll along a canal on the edge of Halesowen before returning to the garden and following winding paths which pass its main features, giving you some idea of its past glories.

The Walk

1. With your back to the canal, take the tarmac track to the left of the Wardens Base building to a T-junction. Turn left along an uphill, tree- and hedge-lined track to a road and continue along it to the A458. Turn left and at a pelican crossing, cross over and take a tarmac track down towards an industrial estate. Continue along a waymarked path that leads off to the right of the track, follow it around a right bend and at a fork by a public footpath sign to Gorsty Hill, take the left hand path down to the canal.

Dudley No 2 Canal was constructed between 1793 and 1798 to provide a link between Dudley and the Birmingham and Worcester Canal at Selly Oak. To the south of Leasowes Park it has now been filled in.

Walk by the canal as far as a footbridge over it and turn right up steps through woodland. Cross a track, keep ahead beside a redundant stile, continue uphill along an enclosed path and at a public footpath sign, turn right over a stile. Walk along a path, climb a stile and keep ahead to emerge once more onto the A458. Cross carefully, turn left for about 50 yards (46m) and at a

Footbridge over the canal near Halesowen

public footpath sign turn right over a stile to re-enter Leasowes Park.

The Leasowes is a hidden and largely unknown gem but ranks as one of Britain's foremost historic gardens, listed by English Heritage on the Grade 1 register of parks and gardens of special historic interest. It was the work of William Shenstone, an 18th century poet, who inherited the

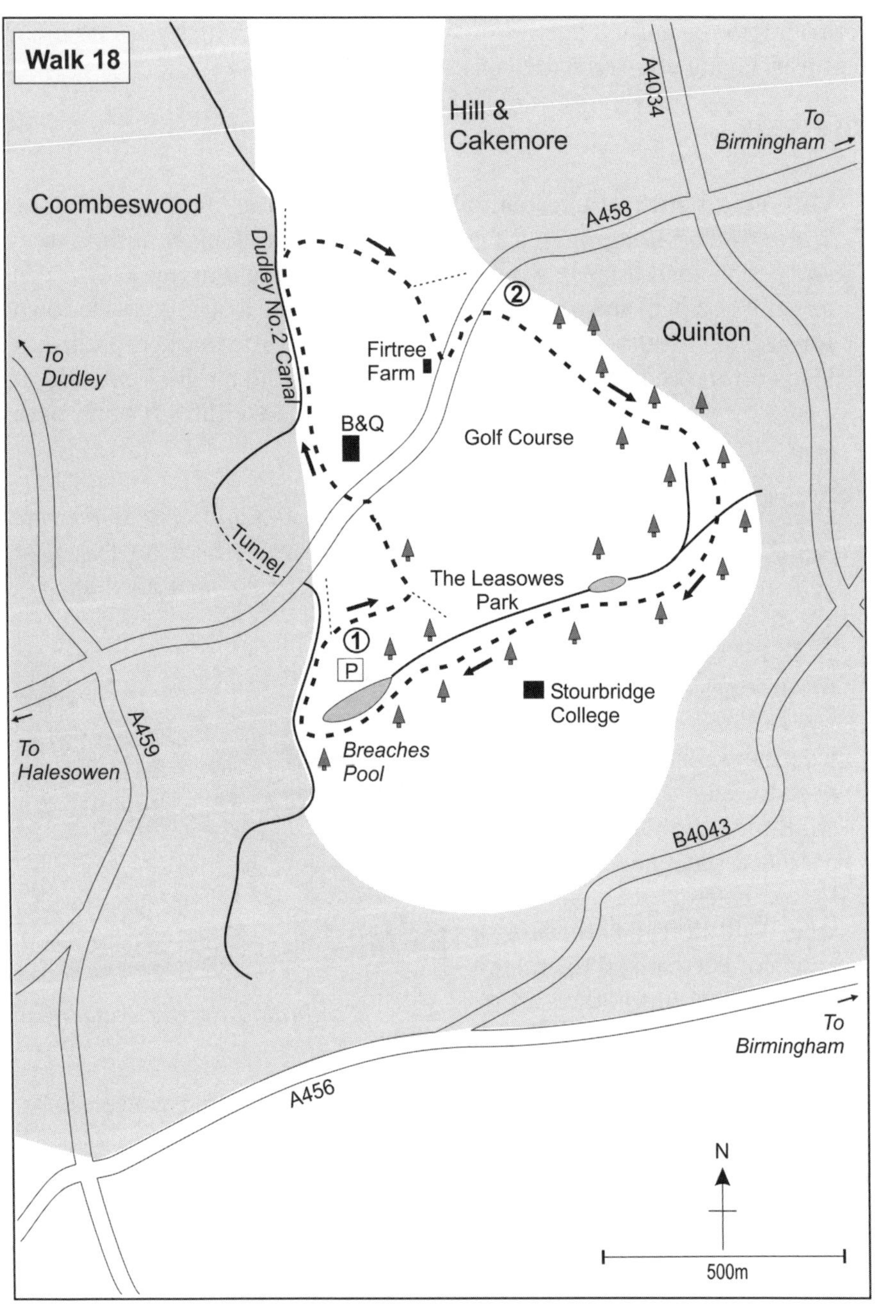

Walk 18
Coombeswood
Hill &
Cakemore
A4034
To
Birmingham
A458
Dudley No.2 Canal
Quinton
To
Dudley
Firtree
Farm
2
B&Q
Golf Course
Tunnel
The Leasowes
Park
1
P
Stourbridge
College
Breaches
Pool
A459
To
Halesowen
B4043
To
Birmingham
A456
N
500m

land in the early 1740s and proceeded to design the garden not on the usual formal lines but in harmony with the landscape. He augmented the streams with pools and cascades, planted trees and shrubs to blend in with the surroundings, placed urns and seats at certain viewpoints and constructed mock ruins, including a medieval priory, to add to the views and improve the overall 'picturesque' qualities of the garden. In conjunction with Lord Lyttleton at nearby Hagley Hall, he was also responsible for the erection of the Four Stones on the Clent Hills to further enhance the views of the hills.

Shenstone died at the early age of 49 but the fame and reputation of his garden increased for a while and attracted many notable visitors. The inevitable decline came in the 19th century. One major development which had an adverse effect on the attractiveness of the garden was the opening of the Dudley No 2 Canal in 1778 which reduced the size of Priory Pool and blocked off many of the views over Halesowen to the Clent Hills. In recent years Dudley Council, the present owners, have carried out some repair work to restore some of the garden's former glories, including the High Cascade and Virgil's Grove, both of which are seen from the walk.

The High Cascade was one of the many features that William Shenstone created at The Leasowes

2. After keeping by a hedge on the right, walk across part of a golf course to enter trees on the far side, pass beside a gate and turn right along

Looking down on Virgil's Grove

a path. At a fork take the right hand path, keeping parallel to the edge of the golf course and heading gently downhill all the while through woodland. The path later bends right and keeps by a stream on the left. After crossing a track, bend left to cross a footbridge and turn right alongside the stream. Then bend first sharply to the left, turn right over another footbridge beside a pool and head gently downhill. Turn right over another footbridge and then turn left down steps beside the recently restored High Cascade, one of Shenstone's picturesque features. Continue by a stream on the left, at a T-junction turn left over a footbridge and the path bends left and then curves right to continue above the attractive if rather gloomy Virgil's Grove. Turn left to descend a flight of steps, cross a footbridge and at a T-junction ahead, take the right hand path, by a pool on the right. Turn right across the end of the pool and take the path on the left, keeping along the right side of the stream. Turn left to recross the stream and turn right onto a path beside the large expanse of Priory Pool. At a T-junction at the corner of the pool, turn right and right again to continue beside it and at the far end climb a flight of steps up an embankment to the canal. Turn right along the towpath for the short distance back to the car park.

Dudley No 2 Canal at The Leasowes

19. Himley Park and the Kingswinford Railway Walk

'A great estate of remarkably variegated surface'

Distance	**5 ½ miles (8.9 km)**
Approximate time	**2 ½ hours**
Start	**Himley Park, off the B4176 just to the east of its junction with the A449 at Himley, grid ref SO890915**
Parking	**Himley Park**
Terrain	**Clear paths and tracks by fields, across parkland and through woodland; almost half the route is on a disused railway track**
Refreshments	**Café at Himley Park**
Public Transport	**Buses from Wolverhampton and Stourbridge**
Map	**Map: OS Explorer 219 (Wolverhampton & Dudley)**

Today we are able to see much more of Himley Park than Elihu Burritt. When he and his companion passed here on their way from Stourbridge to Wolverhampton, they found that 'access to the hall and park was barred by rather rigid restrictions' and had to be content with the view from the road. This route starts by the hall and finishes with a pleasant stroll in the park through woods and by streams and pools. In between, apart from a short stretch of suburban road walking, a former railway track is used, now converted into an attractive footpath and cycleway.

The Walk
The dignified Georgian mansion of Himley Hall has had something of a chequered history. The estate was owned by the Ward family, the Earls of

The handsome façade of Himley Hall

Dudley, and in the early 18th century the modest manor house on the site was demolished and the present grand house was built. At the same time 180 acres of sweeping parkland was created, designed by 'Capability' Brown, with a large lake fed by smaller pools and waterfalls. The landscaping of the park necessitated the moving of the existing Himley village and the building of a new church in 1764.

Proximity to the Black Country and the later encroachment of the noise, smoke and squalor of the local industries caused the family to move further out to Witley Court deep in rural Worcestershire but financial problems caused them to sell Witley and move back to Himley after the First World War. In the 1930s the house became something of a fashionable social centre, visited by the Prince of Wales, later Edward VIII, and his set. After the Second World War it was acquired by the National Coal Board but vacated in the 1960s and the hall and park are now owned by Dudley Council. The splendid park is a popular venue for walkers and the hall is open to the public. It can be hired for private and public functions and frequently hosts various meetings, conferences and seminars.

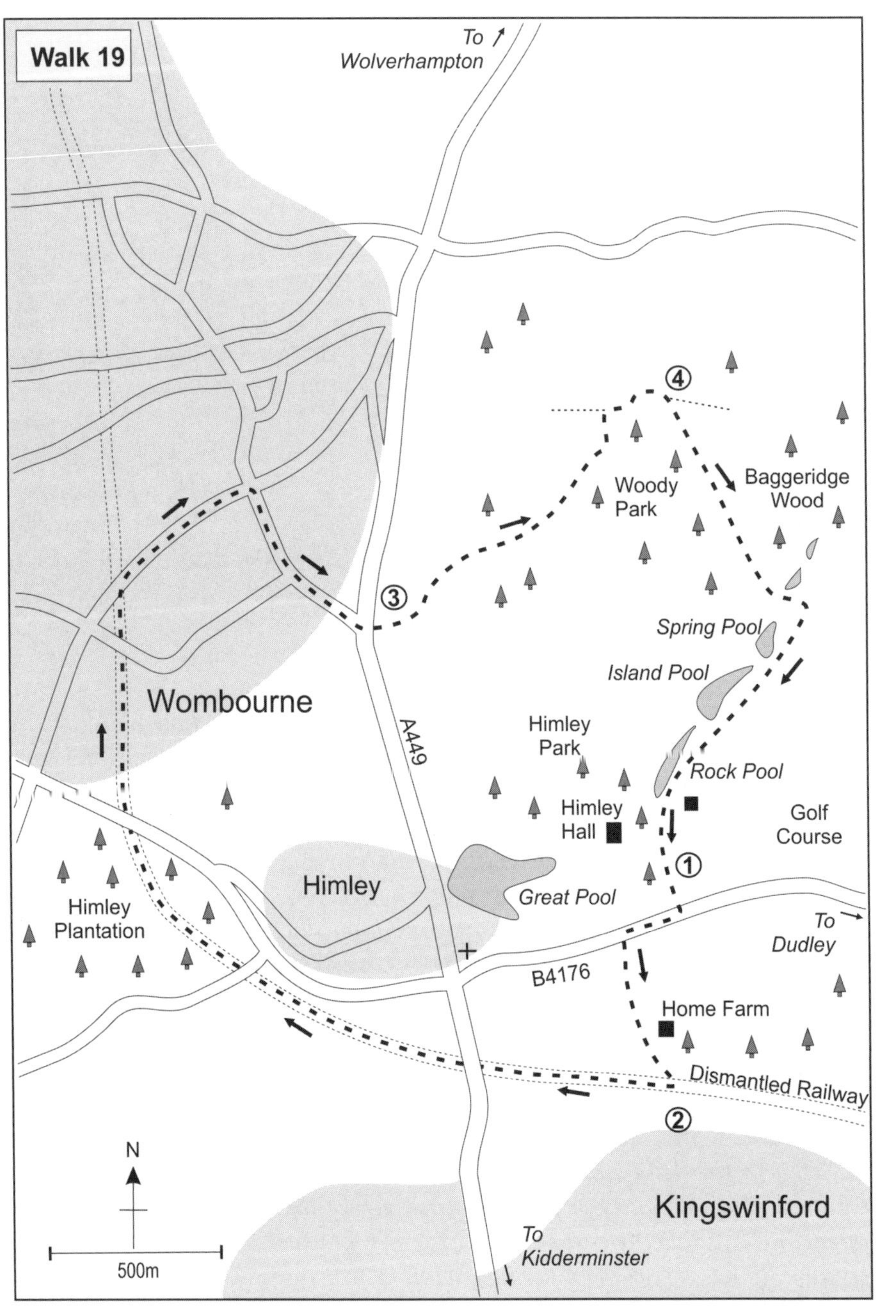

Walk 19
To Wolverhampton
Baggeridge Wood
Woody Park
Spring Pool
Island Pool
Rock Pool
Himley Park
Himley Hall
Golf Course
Wombourne
A449
Himley
Great Pool
To Dudley
Himley Plantation
B4176
Home Farm
Dismantled Railway
N
500m
To Kidderminster
Kingswinford

1. Begin by walking back along the vehicle drive to exit the park and turn right along the road. Look out for a public footpath sign where you turn left along a hedge-lined track, go through a gate and keep ahead to a disused railway bridge. Just before reaching the bridge, turn right, pass beside a barrier and head up to join the former railway track.

   The line was a late addition to the Great Western Railway network, built between 1912 and 1925. It was never commercially successful: passenger services ceased only seven years after the line was completed and it finally closed in 1965. Since then it has been converted into the Kingswinford Railway Walk, a well-used local recreational amenity.

2. Keep along the track for the next 2 miles (3.2 km), passing the remains of Himley station and going through the attractive woodland of Himley Plantation. Where the path bears left to pass through a tunnel and under a bridge, keep ahead up steps and bear right to a road. Continue

Part of the Kingswinford Railway Walk

along it to a T-junction, turn right, in the Wolverhampton direction, heading uphill and follow the road to the A449.

3. Cross carefully to a public footpath sign to Gospel End on the other side and take the narrow path which continues along the right edge of a field. After passing through a belt of trees, walk along the right edge of the next field below sloping woodland on the right and in the field corner, bear right through trees – there is a wall on the right – to emerge into the next field. Continue along its right edge, follow the curve of the field edge first to the left and then to the right and keep ahead to a T-junction. Turn right up to a stile and after climbing it, continue through woodland. At a fork by the ruins of a cottage, take the right hand track which eventually emerges from the trees and heads across a field to a crossways just before the next belt of woodland.

Landscaped pool in Himley Park

4. Turn right along a track, initially along the left inside edge of the trees and later through the wood, heading downhill and curving left to a stile. Climb it, bear right to descend steps, cross a footbridge over a stream and turn right along a track which keeps along the left edge of Spring Pool. Follow the edge of the pool to the right, turn left down steps and continue along the left edge of another pool, Island Pool. Again follow the curve of the pool to the right and at a public footpath sign to Himley Hall, turn left through a kissing gate onto a track. Cross it and keep ahead along a tarmac track to return to the start.

20. Enville and the Sheepwalks

'The grounds far exceeded our conception for extent and artistic embellishment'

Distance	4 miles (6.4 km)
Approximate time	2 hours
Start	Enville, by the war memorial, grid ref SO825868
Parking	Enville
Terrain	Field paths, open hillside, one steady climb, some muddy and overgrown stretches likely on latter part of the route
Refreshments	Pub at Enville
Public Transport	Infrequent buses from Wolverhampton
Map	OS Explorer 218 (Wyre Forest & Kidderminster)

Elihu Burritt really went to town in his praise of the beauty of Enville Gardens, describing what he refers to as 'their relation and value to the Black Country' at the time. In particular he extols the virtues and generosity of the owner of the estate, Lord Stamford, for opening 'this little sequestered world of beauty' to the public on Tuesdays and Fridays through the season where the 'sooty-faced, hard-handed and heavy-shod men of the mine, forge and furnace in all the Black Country may come and luxuriate in these flower gardens without a farthing's charge for admission'. The gardens are no more and the house is not open to the public but this walk takes you across part of the grand parkland of the Enville estate, heading up across the slopes of the Sheepwalks from where the views are both superb and extensive. This walk, little more than a stone's throw from Stourbridge, Dudley and Wolverhampton, illustrates the beauty of the green borderland that surrounds the Black Country at its very best.

The Walk

Even allowing for Burritt's tendency to over-enthusiastic exaggeration, the gardens at Enville Hall must have been a glorious sight throughout most of the Victorian era when they attracted thousands of visitors. The hall itself was reconstructed in the 18th century and the park landscaped at the same time but it was in the second half of the 19th century that the colourful and spectacular gardens were created by the 7th Earl of Stamford. It was the 7th Earl who was particularly praised by Burritt for 'opening up such a great green gallery of exquisite artistry to the masses of the people without money and without price'. He was also praised for building a school for the local village children and for replacing an annual cherry fair, notorious for its cock-fighting, brawling and drunkenness, with a still lively and boisterous but less violent set of sports.

An interesting snippet of information that Burritt acquired from one of the gardeners on the estate was that the working men of the Black Country

Enville Hall

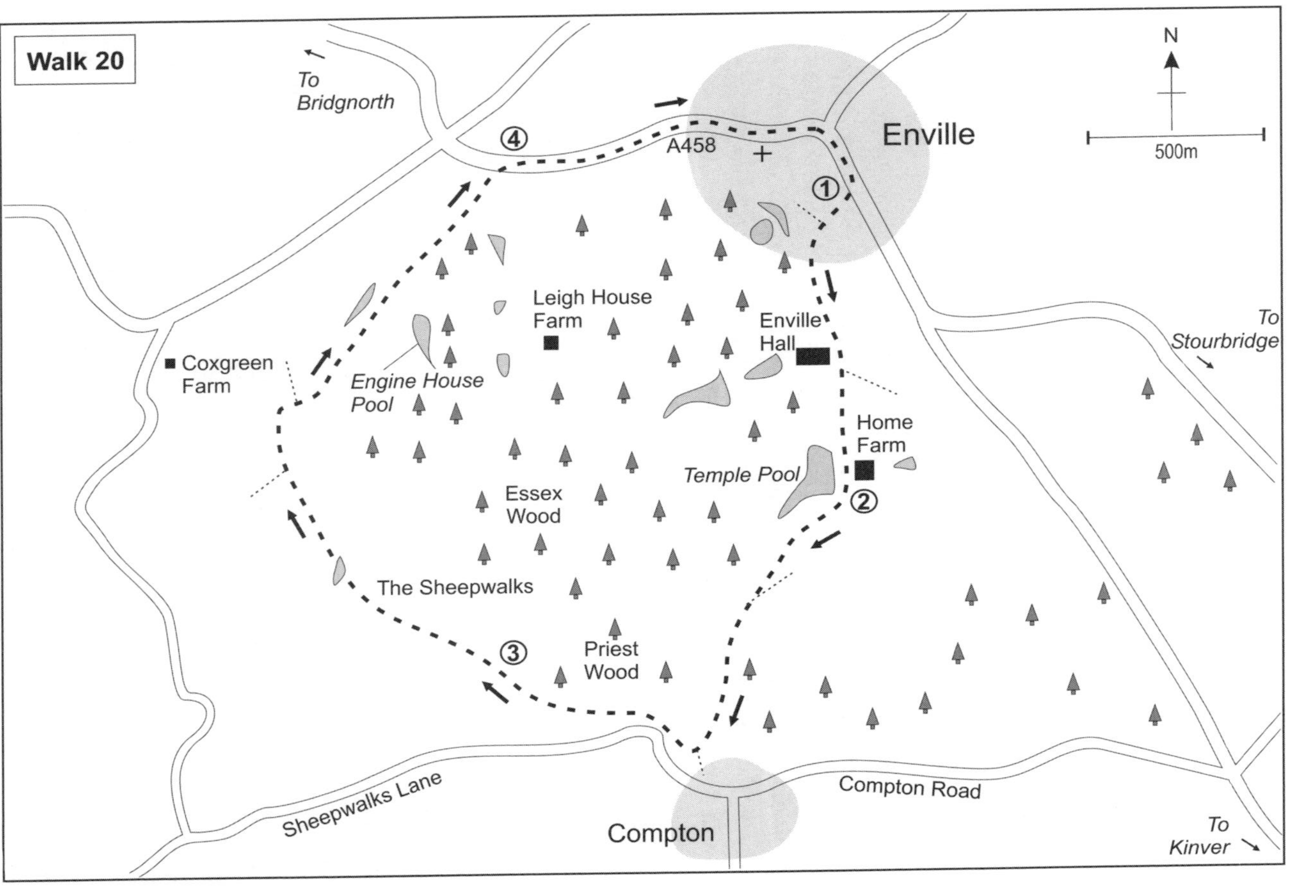
Walk 20
N
500m
To
Bridgnorth
A458
Enville
To
Stourbridge
Coxgreen
Farm
Engine House
Pool
Leigh House
Farm
Enville
Hall
Home
Farm
Temple Pool
Essex
Wood
The Sheepwalks
Priest
Wood
Compton
Sheepwalks Lane
Compton Road
To
Kinver
①
②
③
④

*behaved better than many of the more affluent visitors. According to him
'he could always trust them among the choicest flowers; that they never
overstepped a border that was restricted, and needed no watching. If one
of their number forgot the confidence reposed in them and took a single
step on forbidden ground, he was arrested and reproved in a moment by
his companions'. In contrast 'middle class people, or those who assumed a
superiority over the humble visitors and made less scruple in gratifying
their curiosity......had to be watched with much care to keep them from
trespassing on objects which men of the mine and furnace would not think
of touching'.*

*The gardens were at their peak during the second half of the 19th
century but, following some instances of vandalism, they were closed to the
public in 1892 and since then have never been re-opened on a regular
basis. Nowadays Enville Hall is still a family home and the adjoining
grounds a working estate.*

1. By the war memorial, go through the gates to enter the Enville estate
   and walk along the tarmac drive, later passing a sports field on the left
   and the buildings adjoining Enville Hall on the right. Where the broad
   drive ends just beyond the buildings, climb a yellow-waymarked stile
   and continue across a field, making for a stile in a group of trees on
   the far side. Climb it, keep ahead through the trees – Temple Pool is to
   the right – climb a stile and continue across a field to another one. All
   the way there are fine views behind looking across the pool to the
   façade of the hall. After climbing the stile, keep ahead for a few yards
   to a track.

2. Turn right along it, at a fork, take the left hand track and continue
   across the parkland. After passing a waymarked post, head towards a
   gap between two areas of woodland and just before reaching a gate,
   bear left to a waymarked stile. Climb it and bear slightly left, heading
   uphill across the open grassy slopes of the Sheepwalks.

*From the Sheepwalks there are glorious and extensive views over the
surrounding countryside. Particularly prominent are the Rowley Hills
above the Black Country, the nearby wooded escarpment of Kinver Edge
and, further away, the distinctive profile of The Wrekin.*

Enville Hall from across Temple Pool

Climb a stile near the top, left hand field corner, keep ahead over the brow of the hill and bear right to a waymarked post by the edge of trees. Continue across the top of the hill, following a line of posts until reaching one just to the left of a circle of trees.

3. From here you begin the descent, heading down to the next waymarked post and continuing more steeply down past the next post towards the left of a pool to reach another post. Beyond that cross a footbridge, keep ahead to enter a field and turn right along its right edge. Follow the edge to the left, first heading uphill by a hedge on the right and then continuing gently downhill. Look out for a waymarked post in front of a wooded area where you turn left along a track and at the next post, turn right to continue alongside the left edge of woodland and by the right edge of a field. In the field corner keep ahead between bushes to a waymarked post and turn right along a

narrow path through an avenue of trees, curving left to a stile. This part of the route might become overgrown during the summer months. After climbing the stile, turn right along the right edge of a field, with woodland on the right. When you see a path on the left heading downhill across the middle of a field, turn along it down to a stile. Climb it, turn right, descend steps and continue along a narrow, winding path through woodland above a stream on the left. This path may also get overgrown during the summer. Later turn right up steps and continue through the trees, eventually emerging, via a stile, onto the A458.

4. Turn right and follow it back to Enville, taking care and walking along the verge.

On the edge of the village you pass the church, a fine sandstone building that dates back to the 12th century. It retains many of its medieval

The Sheepwalks

Enville Church

features, including a Norman nave, but was enlarged and much restored in the 19th century. Strangely for someone so interested in old churches, Burritt makes no reference to it.

Also from Sigma Leisure:

Heart of England Way
102 miles of linear walk or 225 miles of 32 linked circular walks
Stephen J Cross

A book both for the long distance and the leisure walker, The Heart of England Way, and 32 circular walks, takes the walker on a journey slicing through the quieter areas of midland, shire, countryside; from the north edge of Cannock Chase, to Bourton on the Water; providing a fascinating view through the back door of the regions history, people, buildings and landscape.
£8.99

Country Walks in and around Warwickshire
Ron Weston

This selection of 32 Warwickshire walks takes you on a journey of picturesque villages and historic churches, stately homes and castles, famous gardens and medieval tracks bound together by a superb network of public footpaths and canal towpaths and sometimes spilling over into adjoining counties. All walks in the book are circular, the longest being $5\frac{1}{2}$ miles and all within a radius of 25 miles from Coventry, with directions of how to get there and where to park.
£8.99

Walks in Herefordshire, Gloucestershire and Worcestershire
Three Choirs Counties
Roy Woodcock

A collection of 30 walks split across the 3 choirs counties, which can boast attractive scenery ranging from the stone villages of the Cotswolds to the flat lands alongside the Severn and extensive woodlands of the Forest of Dean. Includes routes through each of the three county towns, and across many of the best known landscapes as well as visiting several less well known areas

£8.99

Discover The Cotswolds
town and country walks
Roy Woodcock

The 20 walks included in this book are chosen to see a wide range of Cotswold towns and villages and to walk across stunning scenery and visit many historic locations. It has been a particular village, landscape or historic feature which has determined the choice of walks, including such locations as the Roman villa at Chedworth, the old canal at Sapperton, Fairford church, Woodchester Mansion, the amazing water features of the Cotswold Water Park. These walks are not intended to be strenuous. Although a steep hill may be encountered in a few of the walks, for example Wotton-under-Edge, they are mostly gentle walks, and quite short in mileage. The aim is to provide an interesting day out with a short walk, a good lunch in one of the many pubs, and a visit to a feature of interest in the area.

£8.99

Walks around the Malverns
Exploring England's oldest hills and some of the surrounding countryside
Roy Woodcock

The Malvern Hills have well over a hundred miles of paths on the hills and commons, and there is almost unlimited walking with real freedom to roam over many hectares of countryside. The 25 walks were selected to cover the entire range of hills and the adjacent commons; and, as the views looking at the hills can be as impressive as those looking from the hills, a few walks in the Ledbury area to the west and the Upton area and Old Hills to the east have been included.
£8.99

Best Shropshire Walks 2nd Ed
from short strolls to classic rambles
Les Lumsdon

A new revised edition of this much loved guide contains 36 walks, located in all parts of the county. Several walks feature fine hill walking on the Welsh borders and others start from delightful villages and hamlets in the north and east of the county. The Shropshire countryside really comes alive in this well-researched book. All of the walks include stories about the locality: folklore and legends, attractions and facilities. There are clear maps and a selection of photographs to make for an enjoyable and informative read.
£8.99

All of our books are available through booksellers. For a free catalogue, please contact:

Sigma Leisure, Stobart House, Pontyclerc, Penybanc Road, Ammanford SA18 3HP. Tel: 01269 593100 Fax: 01269 596116

info@sigmapress.co.uk   www.sigmapress.co.uk